There's Something About That Chair!

Michael S. Dotson

Published by Michael S. Dotson, 2024.

While every precaution has been taken in the preparation of this book, the publisher assumes no responsibility for errors or omissions, or for damages resulting from the use of the information contained herein.

THERE'S SOMETHING ABOUT THAT CHAIR!

First edition. July 15, 2024.

ISBN: 979-8224434398

Written by Michael S. Dotson.

Table of Contents

Words cannot express how much I sincerely thank all those who have stood by my side with their unwavering commitment during some of the most trying times of my life. For those who have expressed limitless love and patience, provided unconditional support, and invested so much time and energy encouraging and mentoring me over the past 25 years of my life. Your investment in my life will always be remembered, and I am forever grateful for it.

Introduction

The gripping story of the prayer chair began one hot, muggy evening, in the most unlikely of all places, a prison chapel in the far reaches of Northwest Tennessee. When most professing Christians first hear how God is moving in a prison through prayer, their initial reaction is to become shocked with disbelief. Unfortunately, most Christians today look at the incarcerated with disdain and contempt, wondering how God could possibly use social castaways to impact the world. What most of them fail to realize is that over two-thirds of the New Testament Bible was written by the Apostle Paul from a prison cell. While a large part of society views the incarcerated through the colored lens as scripted by the media, God has chosen to use our prisons to heal the brokenness caused by our fallen society, teaching them how to transform their pain into purpose. It is this brokenness; the willingness to become vulnerable and surrender it all to God, I believe, is one of the keys to unlocking the power of God through the prayer chair.

When news of the prayer chair first became known at our facility, many of the prison guards began to mock and scoff at the prisoners who were flocking to the chapel each evening. They even started a rumor that the preacher must be giving away fried chicken in order to get that many people to attend revival each night. What they didn't account for was the power of God moving in the lives of His people. Before long, their disbelief turned into intrigue and even desperation as they began to send prayer requests through some of the inmates. Some would even be so bold as to slip in during the service, pulling the preacher to the side asking for us to pray for them or their family. What started as a joke for many quickly became a source of hope for their lives. Before long, word of the prayer chair spread across the country and even into the far reaches of Bolivia and Zambia, Africa. Prayer requests began to pour in from across the globe and the social castaways that had once been subjugated by society and written off as anti-social deviants had suddenly found a purpose that was impacting the world.

This book tells the gripping story of the prayer chair while revealing the secrets of why God has chosen to use a group of unlikely men to transform the world. Is it as simple as the Apostle Paul suggests in 1 Corinthians 1:27-29, "But God hath chosen the foolish things of the world to confound (put to shame) the wise; and God hath chosen the weak things of the world to confound (put to shame) the things that are mighty; and base (insignificant) things of the world, and things which are despised, hath God chosen, yea, and things which are not, to bring to naught (nothing) things that are: that no flesh should glory in his presence," or have these unlikely men truly discovered the Biblical keys to accessing the power of God through prayer? The power that has healed the broken-hearted, restored broken families, healed the sick, sparked revivals, and caused even their enemies to be at peace with them.

Chapter 1 The Beginning

This story begins some time before the events which led up to the actual conceptualization of the prayer chair. I would regularly walk around the recreation yard during our free time to visit with friends and invite others to church. One particular area on the yard was routinely avoided because it was often frequented by some of the State's most notoriously dangerous inmates. Despite the risk, I would often meander into this area making my way towards the old timers who frequented an old park bench. I would often make small talk with them, listen to some of their tall tales, and then invite them to church. Most would just ignore my invitation or tell me it's too late for God to save them, but for one inmate in particular, this excuse was never enough. This old timer would often jump up out of his wheelchair in protest when invited to church, cussing, berating, and threatening me. I most often laughed and he would grab the footrest on his wheelchair and threaten to hit me with it. I often remember jokingly telling him, "I'm an Appalachian stud, if you hit me with that foot rest it would only break it because my old head is much harder than that old foot rest." Those around us seemed to enjoy the amusement of our daily dance around the bench, watching as I joyfully taunted my old friend. Whether it was the peace of God or the fact that I am 6' 7" weighing 318 pounds, I never felt threatened or scared by our daily dance around that old park bench. Something in my spirit always told me there was a story behind all the pain and anger my old friend was displaying. I vowed to never give up on him since God has never given up on me. As oddly as it sounds, my friend Jerry Cook had grown on me despite having earned the reputation for being one of the most notorious inmates in the history of the Tennessee Department of Corrections. He had become legendary; a figure shrouded in both fear and mystery, his demeanor a reflection of a life scarred by violence and regret.

Like so many others, Jerry's story was one of tragedy and loss, intertwined with the harsh realities of a juvenile delinquent thrown into the unforgiving world of adult prisons during the 60s when juveniles were commonly incarcerated with the rest of the adult population. This would be unheard of today! As one can imagine, being a teenage boy in a prison full of adults, you either learned to be mean and violent or you were exploited and victimized. His descent into darkness accelerated while serving a relatively short sentence for a petty crime. Early one morning, Jerry received word that his niece had been kidnapped and brutally raped. Enraged, angry, and confused, Jerry vowed revenge on the person who hurt his niece. Within days, Jerry had managed to escape from the Old Fort Pillow Prison in Henning, Tennessee. He quickly tracked down the one responsible for hurting his niece and exacted revenge on the man who had viciously brutalized her. Within a few days, law enforcement caught up with Jerry, and he ended up being put on trial and sentenced to more than 150 years in prison. He was told by the judge, "He was never going to see the light of day again," but God had other plans! His primal rage had led him down a path of vengeance and, ultimately, to a fate sealed by a judge's gavel.

One sweltering, muggy afternoon, I made my way over to the old park bench where I found Jerry and the rest of the old timers telling their tall tales. I quickly sensed something was different this time. As I sat and listened, I discovered Jerry had been diagnosed with an aggressive form of terminal cancer, a cruel reminder of mortality's inevitability. After what seemed like an eternity of silence, I looked at Jerry and asked if he was finally tired of running from God and ready to come to church with me. I fully expected to stand toe-to-toe with the devil that day, but instead, a tear rolled down Jerry's face as he said in a very condescending tone of voice, "If I go to church with you, will you leave me alone?" I looked deep into the eyes of my broken old friend and said, "Probably not, but it's a start." I then told him, "I would pick him up at 5:30 on my way to church." Finally, confronted with his mortality, Jerry's heart seemed to soften, his once impenetrable facade crumbling in the face of impending eternity.

Later that evening, as I was heading to church, I saw all the old timers sitting on the bench. I could see Jerry squirming as the rest of the guys poked at him as I drew closer. His apprehension was palpable as he grappled with the demons of his past. I fully expected him to jump out of his wheelchair and take off running across the yard. Surprisingly, he remained glued to his chair, but he was nervous as a house cat in a room full of rocking chairs. As I approached, I never said a word, I just walked around behind him, popped the brake handles on his chair, and off we went to church with Jerry kicking and screaming. All of his buddies laughed and waved goodbye to him. After much protesting, I told Jerry, "A deal was a deal and all you have is your word and you promised to go to church and that was that." Little did the both of us know at the time, but he was fighting a fixed fight and the battle had already been fought and decided in heaven!

As we rolled through the door, we were greeted by Brother Ken Avery, a man I can honestly say has a true heart for God. As Jerry introduced himself to Brother Avery, he began to tell him, "He had been angry with God, had terminal cancer, and all he really wanted was to go home and spend some time with his grandchildren before he died." After a few minutes of socializing, we took our seats at the back of the church. Jerry's first night in church in probably more than fifty years and he had already become a back row Baptist. As the worship services began, the spirit of God started to move through the church. After a few songs, Brother Ken Avery suddenly stood up and announced that God was telling him he had to do something right now! As he walked toward the back of the chapel where the back row Baptist frequented, I could hear Jerry squirming in his wheelchair. Suddenly, Brother Avery's eyes became fixated on Jerry's as he told him, "God wants me to roll you to the front of the church and have everyone gather around and pray for you." As the church gathered around, Jerry began to tell his story and years of anger and bitterness slowly melted away like butter. Through the tears, you could sense the sincerity of his desire to be with his grandchildren. As the church began to pray, you could feel the power of heaven descend upon us as we momentarily basked in God's glory. As the prayers mingled with tears, it washed away decades of bitterness and regret. That night in that hallowed place, the prayer chair was born! What had just transpired defied human logic and reason, a sacred moment where heaven touched earth, and redemption became a tangible reality.

From that point forward, Jerry never missed a church service, and I never had to dance around that old park bench with him again. Jerry's transformation was nothing short of miraculous—a hardened convict softened by the gentle touch of God's love. His newfound faith became a beacon of hope, illuminating the path to reconciliation and forgiveness. With each passing day, Jerry's journey drew closer to its inevitable conclusion, yet his spirit remained unbroken, buoyed by the promise of eternal peace. Within a few weeks of our prayer, Jerry was surprisingly shocked when the parole board contacted him asking if he would like to go home to spend his last days with his family. God had heard the humble cries of the church and miraculously, after more than 51 years in prison, Jerry was able to spend the last three months and three days at home holding his precious grandchildren before he died. Prior to his death, Jerry would call Brother Avery every day and tell him, "Because of you and God, I am the happiest man alive!" And when the time came for him to bid farewell to this old world, he did so with a heart full of gratitude, his final days enriched by the love of family and the solace of faith.

The legacy of the prayer chair lives on—a reminder of God's boundless mercy and the transformative power of redemption. I often reflect on the journey that led to the prayer chair and where my life would be if Brother Ken Avery had not been sensitive to the direction of the Holy Spirit. What if he had refused to obey God's voice? The prayer chair might have never been conceptualized? I am often asked if there is something divinely special about the prayer chair as some would like to believe, or have these unlikely men unlocked the Biblical keys to accessing the power of God through prayer?

Chapter 2 There's Something About That Chair!

I am often asked by cynics and skeptics alike whether there is something divinely special about the prayer chair, or whether there is more to it than simply praying for someone in an old chair. After personally bearing witness to hundreds of answered prayers over the past 15 years, I can emphatically attest there is nothing divinely special about the prayer chair. As disheartening as it is for many who are falsely looking for an object of their faith, the prayer chair is simply a vessel our church has chosen to use as an alter to place ourselves on as we call the church to gather around as we unlock the power of God through prayer. We have chosen a chair instead of kneeling before the traditional church alter simply because many of those we pray for are physically unable to get on their knees to pray. However, they are able to sit in a chair as we pray with them. The power lies in the prayer, not the chair!

The question as to how our church has been able to move God through prayer is a complex, yet powerfully intriguing one. The first question most Christians fail to overcome is how God could possibly use those criminals to impact the world, considering all the selfish harm they have done to others. In order to understand the answer to this question, they must first come to grips with the fact that hurting people often hurt others. Most of these men who have been castigated by society are merely a reflection of the broken homes they derived from. They simply did not have the same opportunities as most and fell through the cracks of our American social system that the Christian Church surrendered to the government over a century ago. At the end of the day, their sin is no greater than anyone else's in the eyes of God. The only difference is they have been arrested and held accountable by our criminal justice system. We would do well to remember, if we see a little speck in someone else's eye, it means that we probably have a plank of timber in our own eye (Matthew

7:3-5). Every wrong we see in others, God finds in us. Every time we judge, we condemn ourselves (Romans 2: 17-24). We must stop using a measuring stick for other people. There's always at least one more fact, which we know nothing about in every person's situation. We should never look down on another person unless we are bending over to help pick them up!

When these men arrive at prison, they are often experiencing a crisis in their lives. It is in this moment of desperation they finally come to grips with the realization they have messed up, hurt others, and have lost everything they once cherished and held important in their lives. Their families, relationships, friendships, job, home, cars, have all been stripped away and every monetary possession they thought defined them as an individual has vanished. Once everything they once loved is lost, it often drives them to a point of brokenness and desperation before God. It is this brokenness, this desperation, which leads these men to repentance and a new life with Jesus Christ. Once the facade of the world has been removed, for the first time in their lives they find themselves free from the bondage of the world and can begin to find their identity, love, and peace in Jesus Christ instead of the worldly possessions that once consumed and defined their lives.

It is this brokenness, this desperation for God where their souls are laid bare, that drives these men to become mighty prayer warriors with the ability to unlock the power of God through prayer. Dr. Charles Stanley's poignant words resonate deeply—"Brokenness is God's requirement for maximum usefulness." In the shattered fragments of their lives, these men find a purity of heart—an unquenchable hunger for God that transcends earthly desires and ambitions. This is why I believe during our deepest and darkest moment of despair, where all the things of this world have been stripped away, is exactly where God finds a pure heart desperately seeking Him. Remember what Jesus said in Matthew 6:24, "No man can serve two masters: for either he will hate the one, and love the other; or else he will hold to the one, and despise the other, Ye cannot serve God and mammon (riches)." It is this hunger and radical desperation for God I believe is one of the keys to unlocking the power of God through the prayer chair.

This is often difficult for many Christians to reconcile, since all they can see is the taint of criminality in the lives of these desperately broken men, but a great answer lies within the word of God itself. In Luke 7, Jesus was invited to dine with a Pharisee at his home, which, during Jesus' time, was the most influential religious sect of the Jewish Sanhedrin. While at the Pharisee's home preparing to dine, a sinful woman showed up at the door unannounced. Many theologians believe this woman was once a prostitute, and she certainly would not have been welcome, particularly in a Pharisee's house, and it took courage for her to come desperately seeking a Savior. She stood at Jesus' feet and began to wash them with her tears, wiping them clean with her hair and then kissed the Savior's feet and anointed them with perfume. The Pharisee, a religious zealot, being full of self-righteous indignation, much like most professing Christians of today, thought if Jesus was truly a prophet, he would have known who this woman was and would never have anything to do with her. Of course, Jesus loved to challenge and turn every religious ritual of the day on its head. Jesus turned to Simon Peter and began to tell a parable in the form of a story about a person who was owed money by two different people. One owed a great sum of money, while the second only owed a little. Since neither of the debtors could afford to pay the creditor back, he forgave them both. Jesus turned and asked Peter, "Which one of these debtors will be the most thankful for their canceled debt?" Peter answered, saying, "I suppose it would be the debtor who owed the most money." Jesus affirmed to Peter that he had indeed answered correctly. Jesus went on to explain, "Wherefore I say unto thee, her sins, which are many, are forgiven; for she loved much: but to whom little is forgiven, the same loveth little" (Luke 7:47). But herein lies the paradox—the depth of one's gratitude is often proportionate to the magnitude of their forgiveness. It is those who have been forgiven much that love much—a truth exemplified by the transformed lives of former outcasts turned prayer warriors.

The difficulty for the Pharisee, just as for much of the modern Church, lies in the inability to accept that God has chosen the most unlikely of men to impact the world through prayer. This prejudice has more to do with the reality that those who were once the chiefest of sinners now have been transformed by the grace of God and developed the radical desire to seek Him because they have been forgiven much more than most Christians. To the world, the outward appearance obscures the true measure of a person's worth. Yet as scripture reminds us, the Pharisee made the same mistake as most modern

Christians do today, by looking at the outward appearance while God is concerned with looking upon the condition of the heart (1 Samuel 16:7). It is this truth that illuminates the path to redemption for all who dare to seek it.

It is this desperation for God that is one of the major keys to unlocking the power of God through prayer. However, there is much more to unlocking the power of prayer than simple desperation for God.

Chapter 3 What Hinders Our Prayers?

In our church, we are extremely blessed to have a dedicated group of preachers who are unashamed of the gospel and hold strong convictions to teach the unadulterated Biblical truths from the Holy Bible without compromise. Unlike most modern churches, our spiritual leaders do not believe in diluting the gospel in order to avoid offending the more sensitive members of the congregation. This commitment ensures we receive pure, uncensored spiritual nourishment, free from the contamination of worldly influences. Since they don't run the risk of offending the churchgoers who despitefully withhold their tithes every time the Word of God steps on one of their secret sins, we have the blessing of receiving the gospel uncensored and unpolluted by worldly influence. These Godly leaders invest deeply in our lives, teaching us not only how to pray but also how to access the transformative power of God through prayer.

Most Christians would readily agree that certain things would hinder them from experiencing an effective prayer life. Most Bible-believing Christians would also acknowledge that prayer is a critically important aspect of their personal relationship with Jesus Christ. Yet, most also admit that their daily lives hinder them from spending time in prayer with the Lord.

Along my journey, I have been taught many Biblical truths that reveal how the presence of sin in our lives can hinder our prayers before God. I strongly believe it is these hindrances that have permeated our churches, preventing them from accessing the full and effectual power of God through prayer. This chapter shares some of these hindrances as well as many of the Biblical truths I have learned along my journey.

BUSYNESS

Many Christians recognize the importance of prayer in nurturing their relationship with Christ, yet they struggle to prioritize it amidst the busyness of daily life. In today's fast-paced society, even if Satan is unable to entice you into living a sinful life, he can still clutter your life with busyness, effectively cutting off your relationship with the Lord. Busyness is one of the greatest enemies to our prayer lives in this technologically advanced society. Even when we are not working or spending time with family, we have the distractions of cell phones, the internet, and all the luxuries and embellishments afforded by the modern world: all designed to keep us busy and distracted. We are always just a click away from a distraction or becoming too busy to spend time with God in prayer. This is one of the greatest blessings of prison. Many of these distractions and busyness from our previous lives have been removed, and we have been significantly slowed down, allowing us more time to grow our personal relationships with Jesus Christ. It is in this moment of solitude in prison, when all worldly distractions are stripped away, we find precious opportunities to deepen our connection with God through prayer.

Scripture offers a timeless lesson on the pitfalls of busyness in the story of contrasts between two sisters, Mary and Martha, in Luke 10. These two sisters of Lazarus lived in the small town of Bethany, just two miles east of Jerusalem. Jesus came to visit them one day, and the scripture tells us Martha became consumed with preparing the perfect meal for Jesus, while her sister Mary chose to sit at the feet of the Savior listening to Him speak instead of helping her. Martha became incensed with her sister for choosing to listen to Jesus instead of helping her. Martha complained, demanding that Jesus tell her to help with the meal preparation. In the end, Jesus commended Mary for seeking spiritual nourishment over the busyness of the world. She is now remembered in scripture for her spiritual desire and discernment, while her sister Martha is remembered for her impatience and excessive concern for mundane things. Similarly, our modern lives teem with distractions, but prioritizing prayer means embracing moments of stillness to commune with God.

If you are too busy to set aside a time each day to get alone with the Lord and pray, then you are too busy! Remember what Jesus said, "...seek ye first the kingdom of God, and his righteousness, and all these things shall be added unto you" (Matthew 6:33). As a word of caution, if you don't make time to talk and fellowship with God, your relationship will suffer and He might readjust your schedule to give you more time to spend with Him.

IDOLATRY

Another hindrance to an effective prayer life is idolatry. This sin was first established with the Ten Commandments when God said in Exodus 20: 3-5, "Thou shalt not have no other gods before me. Thou shalt not make unto thee any graven image, or any likeness of anything that is in heaven above, or that is in the earth beneath, or that is in the water under the earth: Thou shalt not bow down thyself to them, nor serve them…" Often when we read or hear the word "Idol," we immediately think of some stone statue in the Far East or the image of a pagan deity that has been set up in a temple for others to worship and bow too. But the actual concept of idolatry is much more complex than this. While idolatry does stand for the form of prohibited worship of other pagan deities, we are also guilty of idolatry anytime someone or something becomes more significant or more influential in our lives than God Himself. God refuses to play second fiddle to anyone or anything and will not compete for the affections of His children.

For instance, the love of money or material possessions such as extravagant homes, nice automobiles, clothes, jewelry, music, relationships, etc., can all be indicative of idolatry if they eclipse our devotion to God or become more significant than God Himself. Nowadays, sports have definitely become an idolatrous event, especially if you skip church to attend a game. Again, you are forsaking your first love to fulfill the desires of the worldly flesh, which fractures our relationship with Him, obstructing our prayers and impeding our spiritual growth.

This form of idolatry is viewed in scripture as spiritual adultery against God. The Apostle John warned all believers in 1 John 5:21 by saying, "Little children, keep yourselves from idols." It is true that little foxes will spoil the vine. Once your affections have been stolen by something you have developed a love for more than God, your prayer life with Him is severed. This makes it all but impossible to fellowship and communicate with Him through prayer.

LAZINESS

Oftentimes, we become so preoccupied with the things of this world that we fail to find time to pray because we become undisciplined. We end up using our time poorly; failing to understand that wasted time is tantamount to a wasted life. The Bible warns us that laziness will induce a deep sleep, and a lazy person will go hungry (Proverbs 19:15). Overtime, the Bible warns through laziness, a house will begin to leak, and the rafters will begin to decay and the roof will fall in (Ecclesiastes 10:18). We should never become so consumed with our daily lives that we fail to make time to fellowship and talk with the Lord. God wants us to live a life of purpose by using our time wisely and to spend a significant amount of that time with Him. This is why scripture emphasizes the importance of disciplined living and intentional fellowship for the purpose of godliness. This certainly includes spending time in fellowship and prayer with the Lord.

DISOBEDIENCE

When a believer disobeys the Lord, approaching Him in prayer becomes extremely difficult and our relationship suffers as a result. The Bible is consistent in its teaching that God blesses obedience while choosing to punish disobedience. The Apostle John reminds us of this in 1 John 3:22 when he said, "And whatsoever we ask, we receive of him, because we keep his commandants, and do these things that are pleasing in his sight." One of the greatest accomplishments of a believer is when they live a life of purity before God, where they can freely access the power of God through effective prayer. There is definitely a direct connection between obedience to God and successful praying.

While obedience is a choice, so is disobedience against God. As believers, if we choose to do the right thing, the scriptures promise that blessings will follow. For example, when we obediently choose to spend time reading God's word, He blesses us by speaking with us through our spirit and giving His guidance and direction for our lives. When we choose to gather together in the spirit and unity of corporate worship, God promises to manifest Himself in the presence of believers. When we choose to pay our tithes in obedience to His word, He blesses us and provides for all our needs. In contrast, when we are disobedient towards the Lord, He will chastise us and our personal relationship with Him becomes severed and our prayer life becomes exceedingly difficult.

RELATIONSHIPS NOT RIGHT BEFORE GOD

When our relationships with our family and others are not right before God, it will hinder our prayer life. Our Lord cannot answer our prayers as long as we remain angry, bitter, unforgiving, unmerciful, or stubborn towards others. We cannot treat others harshly and then come before the Lord, expecting Him to answer our prayers. Jesus admonished believers in Matthew 5: 23-24 when He said, "Therefore if thou bring thy gift to the alter, and thou rememberest that thy brother hath ought (something) against thee; leave there thy gift before the alter, and go thy way; first be reconciled to thy brother, and then come and offer thy gift." Here, to be reconciled means to be brought back into fellowship or favor with the one we have offended. Jesus makes it abundantly clear that if our relationships are not right before God, then there will be consequences, highlighting the inseparability of healthy relationships and effective prayer.

This same principle also holds true for children who are not honoring their parents according to scripture. The Apostle Paul reminds us to, "Honor thy father and mother: which is the first commandment with promise" (Ephesians 6:2). I strongly believe that God intended for this commandment to extend beyond the time in which a child is still under the authority of their parents. I think it continues throughout our entire lives. If we obey this commandment, God promises to make our lives long and prosperous. Just think, if our children don't learn to honor their parents, the disrespect will spill over into their adult lives, affecting every other relationship, including their relationship with God. When they have their own children, the problem accelerates into the next generation. Soon, our entire society is plagued with disrespect in our homes, our schools, our workplaces, and in our churches. The Lord can certainly not tolerate this type of rebellion in the lives of believers.

When your marital relationship is not right before God, your prayers will also be hindered. Scripture reveals to us in 1 Peter 3:1-7 the balanced approach God desires for all marital relationships. In fact, the Apostle Peter specifically warns us that, "Likewise, ye husbands, dwell with them according to knowledge, giving honor unto thy wife, as unto the weaker vessel, and as being heirs together of the grace of life; that your prayers be not hindered" (1 Peter 3:7). Marriage is God's perfect picture of how the church ought to relate to Jesus. According to Ephesians 5:22-23, Jesus is the husband, and the church is the wife. All men are to lead their families in a loving manner, just as Christ loves and leads His church. Wives are to submit to their husbands with respect, just as the church does to Christ. Your relationships must be right with your spouse in order for God to hear and answer your prayers, because in a covenant of marriage, two people are made one and are regarded as one flesh before God. Your prayers must be one that honors and considers your spouse. In the absence of right relationships before God, your prayers will be hindered.

UNFORGIVENESS

Unforgiveness is one of the biggest hindrances to an effective prayer life. Anytime we become angry and fail to forgive, that anger continues to manifest itself until it eventually poisons our hearts with bitterness and resentment. When we harbor bitterness and unforgiveness in our hearts, the Lord turns a deaf ear to our prayers. Jesus gave us some sobering words when He said, "For if ye forgive their trespasses, your heavenly Father will also forgive you: but if ye forgive not men their trespasses, neither will your father forgive your trespasses" (Matthew 6:14-15). In other words, we are commanded to forgive, because we are forgiven, underscoring its indispensable role in fostering healthy relationships with God and others.

Unforgiveness has, and always will be, a sensitive subject to all of us who have been offended or harmed by others, especially when it occurred in our childhood causing physical, mental, and emotional trauma that can last a lifetime. Being incarcerated for more than 25 years, I have first-hand experience witnessing the devastating impact unforgiveness has on the lives of broken men, as well as the damage their pain has caused in the lives of crime victims.

Speaking from first-hand experience, in 1997, as an angry, selfish young person, I accidentally took another person's life and justly earned my place in prison. Several months after this occurred; the victim's wife approached my girlfriend's mother at the local county fair asking questions about me and what had occurred. At the time, I could not speak with her due to my ongoing involvement with the criminal justice system. As time went on, I could tell that she was becoming angry and confused, not knowing what really happened on that tragic day. A few years later, I received word that she was still struggling to find answers. I finally reached out to her through my girlfriend's mother because I thought she rightly deserved to hear the truth about what happened. Not only was I blessed with the opportunity to share the truth of what had occurred, but I also had the opportunity to ask for forgiveness and share with her why I felt it was so important for her to forgive me. I shared with her the principal of forgiveness I had learned that freed me from the bondage of anger and bitterness in my own life. It is important to understand that forgiveness has a much more far-reaching effect than merely hindering your prayer life. Often times, every pain and emotion we experience is rightly justified, and forgiving the one who offended us does not mean we are letting someone off the hook for what they have done. Their forgiveness is inconsequential to the pain we may be experiencing. Nothing can replace the eternal void or pain that may be present in our lives. Forgiveness is not about the one who may have offended us, but about us! For as long as we continue to harbor anger and resentment towards others, they will continue to maintain a certain measure of control over our lives. We do not deserve to see these unfortunate events continue to maintain control over our emotions and life. If we do, it can destroy us through bitterness!

As I shared my own story and journey to forgiveness, I could tell it was having an impact in her life. Although the forgiveness I was blessed to experience from my victim's wife had absolutely nothing to do about me, it freed her from the bondage of anger and bitterness that had consumed her life for several years. Forgiveness is never an easy thing to do, and it is something we may have to do daily for several years before we finally experience a breakthrough.

Experiencing forgiveness gives you permission to release all the anger, resentment, and bitterness that has characterized your life since your life-altering experience. This is extremely important because bitterness is a substance like an acid that can eat its own container from the inside out. When we become bitter and refuse to forgive those who have offended us, it destroys us physically and emotionally as well as short-circuits our prayers. Jesus gave us one of the greatest examples of forgiveness that has ever been witnessed. Even after Jesus had been falsely arrested and accused of a crime He was innocent of, He was tried, convicted, and sentenced to death on the cross. If this wasn't enough, prior to His crucifixion, He was stripped, beaten to the point of being unrecognizable, and then dressed in a robe with a crown of thorns shoved on His head, spit on, struck in the face, mocked, abused, and publically humiliated for all to see. And if this wasn't enough, He was forced to bear the burden of carrying His cross to the place where He was publically murdered. Despite all of this, in Luke 23:34, Jesus cried out, "Father, forgive them, for they know not what they do." Wow! If Christ, for our sakes, forgave those who were crucifying

Him, surely we can muster enough strength to forgive those who have offended us. Remember, Jesus made it clear if you refuse to forgive other people who have wronged you, God will refuse to forgive you severing your prayer life with the Lord.

UNCONFESSED SIN

Unconfessed sin will have a detrimental impact on our lives, impeding our prayers and stifling our spiritual vitality. If we harbor unconfessed sin in our hearts, God will not even hear our prayers, effectively cutting off all communication with the Lord. Scripture confirms this in Psalm 66:18, "If I regard iniquity in my heart, the Lord will not hear me."

I know this may sound like breaking news to some, but every Christian sins after they are saved and become a believer in Jesus Christ. When a Christian sins, they do not lose their salvation, but they can lose the joy of their salvation. Just like leaves that clog a gutter preventing the water from flowing down the spouts and away from the foundation of a house, sin clutters and clogs up our prayer life, preventing the Lord from being able to hear and answer our prayers. In order for this severed relationship to be restored and the anointing of the Holy Spirit to begin flowing again in our lives, we must humble ourselves and confess and repent of our sins. Scripture tells us in Proverbs 28:13, "He that covereth his sins shall not prosper: but whoso confesseth and forsaketh them shall have mercy." This could not be any clearer that God refuses to hear the prayers of Christians who harbor unconfessed sin in their lives. This is often difficult because many Christians struggle with that entangling sin which seems to remain persistent in our lives, but Hebrews 12:1 says, "...let us lay aside every weight, and the sin which doth so easily beset (ensnare) us, and let us run with patience the race that is set before us." These types of entangling sins are often different for each individual Christian, but regardless of what type of sin it is, it will sever your personal relationship with the Lord.

We must learn to get alone with the Lord in prayer, asking Him to reveal to us any unconfessed sin in our lives which we have not yet repented of in order to restore our relationship with Him. A great scriptural example of this is when David lusted after Bathsheba and found himself involved in an extramarital affair which ended in murder. After suffering the punishment of losing his newborn child, David prayed, "Search me, O God, and know my heart: try me, and know my thoughts, and see if there be any wicked way in me, and lead me in the way everlasting" (Psalms 139:23-24). As long as unconfessed sin remains in the life of a Christian, the Holy Spirit will gently and specifically reveal it. If they refuse to deal with it, they will be unable to move forward in their relationship with the Lord until they have dealt with it. If there is any unconfessed sin in your life, confess it as sin, repent of it, and ask God to forgive you. Then claim His promise of unconditional forgiveness by faith. Afterwards, get alone with God, asking Him to, "Restore unto me the joy of my salvation; and uphold me with thy free spirit." (Psalm 51:12). Humble and sincere confession and repentance pave the way for restoration, renewing our fellowship with God and reinvigorating our prayer life. If you want to experience a powerful and effectual prayer life, then you must get rid of your unconfessed sin!

WAVERING FAITH

God does not want us to pray just for the sake of it. He desires for us to pray in faith, believing we will receive what we ask for in prayer, as doubt and uncertainty erode our confidence in God's ability to answer prayer. Scripture underscores God's desire for a prayer of faith, which lies in the story of two blind men following Jesus crying out to have mercy on them. Jesus asked if they believed He could heal them and they earnestly responded "Yes, Lord." Jesus then responded by saying, "According to your faith, be it unto you" (Matthew 9:29). This is a profound statement from Jesus Himself, revealing that prayer is answered according to our faith. This principal of prayer was expounded on even further by James, the half-brother of Jesus when he said, "If any of you lacks wisdom, let him ask of God, that giveth to all men liberally, and unbraideth not, and it shall be given him. But let him ask in faith, nothing (not doubting) wavering, for he that wavereth (doubts) is like a wave of the sea driven with the wind and tossed. For let not that man think that he shall receive anything of the Lord. A double-minded man is unstable in all his ways" (James 1:5-8). This makes it clear that prayer and faith are inseparable and must be exercised as one.

God has little regard for wavering faith, especially a faith that says, "Maybe God will decide to answer my prayer, but perhaps He won't." This is the unstable faith that James was speaking about as an unstable wave of the sea. For many Christians, this lack of faith is often caused by allowing their emotions to control their lives. As they ride the daily roller-coaster called emotions, one day they claim to feel the strong presence of God and they experience joy and peace. The next day, when they are faced with some adversity or feeling depressed, they say that God is nowhere to be found and must not care about them. This often leaves them feeling abandoned, which can lead to becoming resentful and even bitter towards God. But God has promised, "I'll never leave thee, nor forsake thee" (Hebrews 13:5). This type of unstable emotional temperament is the same as being tossed about like wind-driven waves upon the sea.

Our personal relationship with the Lord cannot be based on how we might feel on any given day. Feelings come and go and emotions change, but God's word will stand firm forever! Our prayers must be grounded in the Word of God, not based on our own personal feelings or emotions.

There are several scriptural instances in the Bible that clearly teach that God was moved in a particular situation simply because someone prayed in faith and believed God would act on their behalf. For instance, King Hezekiah fell ill and the prophet Isaiah told him to, "Set thine house in order; for thou shalt die, and not live" (2 Kings 20:1). Had King Hezekiah become driven by his emotions, he probably would have spiraled into a deep state of depression and eventually succumbed to his illness. Instead, he laced up his prayer boots and got alone with God and cried out to Him in faith, believing He would heal him. God heard King Hezekiah's prayer and turned the prophet Isaiah around, sending him back to the King. God told Isaiah to tell King Hezekiah, "Thus saith the Lord, the God of David thy father, I have heard thy prayer, I have seen thy tears: behold, I will heal thee: on the third day thou shalt go up unto the house of the Lord" (2 Kings 20:5). Now, God did not say, I had already decided to heal you according to my predetermined providence, but I just wanted to make you sweat it out. No, God heard Hezekiah's faith-filled prayer and then decided to heal him according to his faith.

Others, like Elijah, also made prayers of faith, asking God to shut up the windows of heaven for over three years and six months. After this time, Elijah prayed again, and the heavens were opened and it rained (James 5:17-18). Imagine if we developed a radical, faith-filled prayer life like this. Oh, how we would could change the world!

When we pray, God must be the sole object of our faith. He refuses to compete with anyone or anything else for our affections or prayers. Remember, "...without faith it is impossible to please him: for he that cometh to God must believe that he is, and that he is a rewarder of them that diligently seek Him" (Hebrews 11:6). Not only can we not please Him without faith, but anything that "...is not of faith is sin" (Romans 14:23). This is why all Christians are commanded to "...walk by faith, not by sight" (2 Corinthians 5:7).

Not only are we saved by faith, but we are to walk and pray by faith. Obviously, faith is the missing ingredient in most Christians struggling to experience an effective prayer life. This is why it is so important to read your Bible daily, learn of God's purposes, and then believe He will answer your prayers according to your faith. Without faith, your prayer life will be hindered.

PRAYERS ARE INDIFFERENT TO GOD'S WORD

Many Christians may not understand and it may sound counterintuitive to many of them, but in order to have an effective prayer life, you must be serious about reading the Word of God and applying it to our daily lives. It is impossible for you to live with a closed Bible while simultaneously expecting to have an effective prayer life. The Bible is one of the principal means by which God chooses to speak to the New Testament Church. The Bible is God's revealed will and His manual for right living. I once heard an acronym for the Bible is: *B*asic *I*nstruction *B*efore *L*eaving *E*arth. I have found this to be personally true because it contains God's promises relating to prayer; it holds God's commandments for how we are to receive and use God's blessings and defeat our enemies.

It is impossible to turn a deaf ear to the word of God and then attempt to approach God in prayer, expecting Him to answer them. The Bible has both wisdom and inspiration that we need for our daily walk with God while present here on earth. If we read the word of God daily, it will provide insights into how we are to pray, so they will align with the word of God. Unless you take daily reading of the word of God seriously and make sure your prayers align with the Bible, your prayers will be hindered.

SELFISH MOTIVES

Often we find ourselves praying that God would bless us with something that is totally a selfish, self-serving request. James, the half-brother of Jesus, examined such types of selfish motives when he said, "Ye ask, and receive not, because ye ask amiss that ye may consume it upon your lusts" (James 4:3).

All our actions are either aimed at glorifying God, or they are aimed towards fulfilling our fleshly desires. Our motives are to either exalt ourselves or to bring glory to almighty God.

Anytime our prayers have been hindered, we should get alone with God asking Him to reveal to us what is hindering our prayers. Anytime we are looking to God to answer our prayers we should ask Him to, "Clarify our thoughts and sift our motives that our prayers may be pure before Him." If there is any doubt as to our motivation we should ask these questions, "Why am I asking God for this certain thing," "Is the motivation to make me feel or look better, or get me noticed or praised by other people," "Or is it so we might help others or move towards fulfilling God's plan, purpose, and destiny for our lives?" We should also examine our prayers to make sure they line up with the word of God, because He will never bless us with something that is contrary to His word. God will also never answer our prayers unless He is certain we will be good stewards of the things He gives us and that we will share them with others.

When praying for a blessing, God fully expects all believers to be generous to those who are less fortunate than we are. Many of God's blessings in the Bible are specifically reserved for those who take care of the poor, widows, and orphans. We must use what God has blessed us with to bring about equity and justice for those who are struggling and are helpless to obtain the basic essentials to survive.

As long as our motives before Him are pure, He promises to bless us, but if our motives are to fulfill our fleshly desires, it will hinder our prayer life.

FAILURE TO TITHE

One of the most common Biblical errors Christians can do to hinder their prayer lives is failing to tithe. God absolutely refuses to tolerate stinginess—whether it's directed towards Him or towards others. If God does not seem to be answering your prayer requests for financial or material needs, then you should check your motives and your giving. If your finances never seem to be adequate enough to cover your expenses, then check your giving.

The principal of tithing was established for all believers and God will not violate this cycle of giving and receiving. The more you give to God, the more He will bless you if it is done with a pure heart and the proper motives. God's law of tithing requires reciprocity! One of Brother Ken Avery's favorite sayings is, "God will give through you what He will not give to you." I promise, you can't out give God!

The scripture affirms this principle when it says, "Bring ye all the tithes into the storehouse, that there may be meat (food) in mine house, and prove (test) me now herewith, saith the Lord of hosts, if I will not open you the windows of heaven, and pour you out a blessing, that there shall not be room enough to receive it" (Malachi 3:10).

God's warnings and promises are clear when it comes to the law of tithing. Failing to tithe according to His commands will hinder your prayer life. Be bold enough to test His promises and He will pour out His blessings before you.

CONCLUSION

Hindrances to an effective prayer life often overlap, making it increasingly difficult to identify what might be hindering our prayers. This is why it is important to get alone with God daily asking Him to, "Clarify our thoughts and sift our motives that our prayers may be pure before Him." By reading the word of God daily and examining your heart and the motivation that drives it, you can avoid the hindrances that sever your prayer life before God. This will allow you to come before Him with a pure heart, allowing you to experience the power of God through prayer. I promise it will transform your life, your family, your church, and your community. Be bold enough to try it

Chapter 4 Prayer Enhancers!

Many believers ask if there is anything we can do as a body of Christ to enhance our prayer lives? The simple answer to this question is absolutely! Many of the keys to enhancing our prayer lives are revealed in the word of God. Just as we have hindrances to our prayers, there are also Biblical insights and principals that can revolutionize the way we pray. I believe it is important for me to share many of the prayer insights and principals I have learned throughout the years to enhance my prayer life. The more believers who learn these principals and pass them on to their children and grandchildren, the more impact we can have on our families, our churches, our communities, and our world.

THE HOLY SPIRIT

The Holy Spirit is often referred to in the scriptures as our "Helper." In fact, Jesus said, "...I will pray to the Father, and He shall give you another Comforter (helper), that He may abide with you forever; even the Spirit of truth; whom the world cannot receive, because it seeth Him not, neither knoweth Him: but ye know Him; for He dwelleth with you, and shall be in you." (John 14: 16-17). The Holy Spirit, who dwells inside every believer, will guide, direct, and warn us in every aspect of our daily walk with God. This includes working to enhance our prayer lives.

The Apostle Paul gave us some wonderful insight into the interworking of the Holy Spirit when he said, "Likewise the Spirit also helpeth our infirmities (weaknesses): for we know not what we should pray for as we ought: but the Spirit itself maketh intercession for us with groanings which cannot be uttered. And he that searcheth the hearts knoweth what is the mind of the spirit, because he maketh intercession for the saints according to the will of God" (Romans 8:26-27). Even when we don't know what to pray for, the Holy Spirit of God steps in and prays for us according to God's will for our lives. We must take notice, though; the Spirit of God searches our hearts to know what the mind of the spirit is, so in order to maintain an effective prayer life our hearts must remain pure before God!

How much must God care about us and the importance of our prayer lives to give us a Helper willing to come alongside us to help lift the heavy burdens of life? How wonderful it is to have the Holy Spirit who stands on the other side of our prayer burden, reaches down alongside us, and picks up our burdens, and lifts them up to our Father in Heaven. The Holy Spirit then turns our prayer into a request that is holy and acceptable before an almighty God that He can answer!

PRAYING SCRIPTURE

During my early years of incarceration, I was encouraged by one of our prison chaplains to begin memorizing scripture verses from the Bible. I was especially encouraged to memorize verses that addressed my areas of weaknesses, where I was struggling to gain victory in my life. These weaknesses are different for every Christian, but I promise you there are specific scriptures that can help with your daily walk with God. I also took time to memorize scriptures of many of God's promises to all believers, especially those where God promised to answer our prayers. I soon found myself praying those same scripture verses back to God as I was facing those particular temptations, even reminding Him of His promises to answer my prayers according to His word. When I did, I found that the power and authority of God was present in my prayers like never before!

Jesus said, "If you abide in Me, and My words abide in you, ye shall ask what ye will, and it shall be done unto you" (John 15:7). As long as the word of God abides in us, our prayers become more effective and powerful. God's will is always found in His Word. This is why it is so important to read the Word of God daily and search out the scriptures for His revealed will. Anytime we pray according to the Word of God, we are praying according to the will of God. God then hears our prayers and is obligated to answer them. The Apostle John revealed this to us when he said, "...this is the confidence that we have in him, that, if we ask anything according to his will, he heareth us: and if we know that he hear us, whatsoever we ask, we know that we have the petitions that we desired (asked) of him" (I John 5:14-15). Wow, what a promise! God has plainly told us if we pray the word of God to Him with a clear heart and a submissive attitude towards His will, He is obligated to answer our prayers. Praying the word of God is definitely a prayer enhancer!

PRAYING IN JESUS NAME

The name of Jesus carries authority both in heaven and on earth. There is great scriptural support for praying in the authority of Jesus' name since Jesus Himself said, "...whatsoever ye shall ask in my name, that will I do, that the Father may be glorified in the Son" (John 14:13). What Jesus meant was anytime we pray according to God's will; He will grant our request when we pray in Jesus' name. When Jesus said to, "Ask in His name," He was instructing us to offer our prayers based upon His divine authority, not ours.

There is great scriptural support for the authority of Jesus' name. In fact, even Satan and his demons understand and submit to this authority. In Acts 16, the Apostle Paul and Silas were traveling to the temple to pray, and they ran into a young slave girl who was possessed by an unclean spirit. This young girl was being exploited by her masters as a story-teller. The unclean spirit that possessed the young girl was able to recognize the presence of God in the lives of Paul and Silas, and she followed them around crying out, "...these men are the servants of the most high God, which shew unto us the way of salvation" (Acts 16:17). Now this young girl did this for several days and it became annoying to the Apostle Paul so one day he turned to the possessed girl and spoke to the unclean spirit and said, "...I command thee in the name of Jesus Christ to come out of her. And he came out the same hour" (Acts 16:18). There are several things that you should recognize about this event. First, the Apostle Paul spoke to the unclean spirit, not the woman; second, he commanded the spirit to leave her, rather than merely requesting the spirit to leave her; and third, he commanded her, "In the name of Jesus Christ." The Apostle Paul had no authority to command the unclean spirit to leave the young girl apart from the authority of Jesus' name!

When I was 18 years of age, I wanted to buy a new car but I did not have enough money to purchase it with cash. I decided I would go to the local bank and ask for a loan. I set up a meeting with a loan officer, thinking I would not have any trouble getting the loan. Despite having stellar credit, the loan officer asked me, "What type of collateral I had to offer to cover the loan?" When I replied, "Nothing," they said, "Then we cannot loan you any money to purchase a car unless you have adequate collateral." Before I left, the loan officer did tell me, "Although I could not get a loan on my own, I could get a loan if I can get my father to co-sign the loan for me." This is when I discovered even though I could not get a loan in my name, I could get one in my father's name.

Even when we have no authority to receive something from our Heavenly Father in our own names, we can instead receive it based on the authority of Jesus' name. Since Jesus died on the cross for our sins, our debt has been paid in full. We are now in an eternal covenant with our Lord through Jesus Christ. Even though we may not have much collateral saved up in heaven's bank, through the name of Jesus, we have all the collateral we need. As long as we pray in the authority of Jesus' name, we can enjoy the benefits of answered prayer.

CONDITION OF THE HEART MATTERS

The condition of a believer's heart matters in the sight of an almighty God. Anytime we come before Him in prayer, not only must we approach His throne of grace with a pure, clean heart, but He is also seeking a humble, hungry, and holy heart. A great scriptural example of God's desire for the condition of our hearts was revealed when He said, "...the Lord seeth not as man seeth; for man looketh on the outward appearance, but the Lord looketh on the heart" (1 Samuel 16:7). Attention all Christians, the condition of the heart matters!

A HUMBLE HEART

God demands we approach His throne of grace with a humble heart, because He has declared, "...my glory will I not give to another, neither my praise to graven images" (Isaiah 42:8). This is why God wants all believers to approach Him in prayer with an attitude and a spirit of humility.

Isaiah was called by God to begin his prophetic ministry and saw the Lord in a vision. God was exalted high, sitting on His throne, clothed in glory that filled heaven's temple while the angels sang about His holiness. Isaiah was so overwhelmed with the glory of almighty God that he cried out, "Woe is me! For I am undone (destroyed); because I am a man of unclean lips, and I dwell in the midst of a people of unclean lips: for mine eyes have seen the King, the Lord of hosts" (Isaiah 6:5). This is the deep act of contrition and humility God desires from us when we come before His throne of grace.

God desires for us to approach His throne of grace in prayer with a spirit of humility and meekness. In fact, "...God resists the proud, and giveth grace to the humble. Humble yourselves therefore under the mighty hand of God, that he may exalt you in due time" (1 Peter 5:5-6). It was our sins, yours and mine, that nailed Jesus to the cross, and we should have enough respect to approach Him with the humility He deserves. He is our holy, exalted, Creator and sustainer of the entire universe! A wise man once said, "Make sure when you pray that you make yourself little and God big!" In fact, make sure you make yourself little enough that God can use you as a mighty prayer warrior for His glory!

A HUNGRY HEART

God desires a desperate and hungry heart when we come before His throne of grace. The prophet Jeremiah revealed this to us when he said, "For I know the thoughts that I think toward you, saith the Lord, thoughts of peace, and not of evil (calamity), to give you a future and an expected end. Then shall you call upon me, and ye shall go and pray unto me, and I will hearken (listen) unto you. And ye shall seek me, and find me, when ye shall search for me with all your heart" (Jeremiah 29:11-13). God's desire is for us to pray with all our hearts. The Lord loves desperate, passionate prayers. The author in the book of Hebrews revealed that Jesus often prayed this way, ""...in the days of His flesh, when he had offered up prayers and supplications with strong crying and tears unto him that was able to save him from death, and was heard in that he feared..." (Hebrews 5:7). Praying is not always about remaining calm, dignified, and peaceful. Sometimes prayer must become more like birthing a baby than a quiet conversation in a public library. No wonder Jesus instructed us to go into our prayer closet when we pray in private. It is not meant for everyone to hear us when we are having a Holy Ghost fit before the altar of God! God does not want us to become weak, worldly Christians; He wants us to fight with the passion of a heavyweight champ! If you can scream and shout with such fervor at a football game, why not before the throne of grace?

God also does not desire or hear prayers that last forever with meaningless verbiage. In fact, Jesus said, "But when ye pray, use not vain repetitions, as the heathen do: for they think they shall be heard for their much speaking. Be not ye therefore like unto them: for your Father knoweth what things ye have need of, before ye ask him" (Matthew 6:7-8). God does not desire, nor can He bless a phony ritual! He is seeking a sincere and passionate personal relationship with us. Remember, God listens to a hungry heart!

A HOLY HEART

God demands we come before His throne of grace with a holy heart. David, a man God said was, "...a man after His own heart," asked, "Who shall ascend into the hill of the Lord? Or who shall stand in his holy place" (Psalm 24:3)? David then answered his own question when he said, "He that hath clean hands, and a pure heart; who hath not lifted up his soul unto vanity, nor sworn deceitfully? He shall receive the blessing from the Lord, and righteousness from the God of his salvation" (Psalm 24:4-5). Christians cannot live a sinful and rebellious life and expect God to hear and answer our prayers. God is a holy God, and He demands that His children walk in His holiness as well.

These scriptures emphasize all that I have been saying, that it is important for all believers to maintain a spirit of clean hands and a pure heart before God, lest our prayers be hindered. It is God who must do the cleansing and purifying if we are to come before His throne of grace. Only after we have been cleansed and purified by an almighty God can we receive His blessing.

Sin eternally separates sinners from a Holy God. This is confirmed by the Prophet Isaiah when he said, "Behold, the Lord's hand is not shortened, that it cannot save; neither his ear heavy, that it cannot hear: But your iniquities have separated you and your God, and your sins have hid his face from you, that he will not hear" (Isaiah 59:1-2). It is only through the atoning sacrifice of our Lord and Savior Jesus Christ that we can come before the throne of grace with a holy heart. God has promised, "If we confess our sins, he is faithful and just to forgive us our sins, and to cleanse us from all unrighteousness" (1 John 1:9). Only then can we approach His throne of grace with a holy heart.

PRAYING TOGETHER

There is something special that occurs when we gather together as a church around the prayer chair in unity of spirit. It's as if a piece of heaven falls down upon us and you can sense the very presence of God as we pray. Jesus gave us a clue as to what was happening in Matthew 18:19-20 when he said, "Again I say unto you, that if two of you shall agree on earth as touching anything that they shall ask, it shall be done for them of my father which is in heaven. For where two or three are gathered together in my name, there am I in the midst of them." In these verses, Jesus was speaking in the context of disciplining sinful members of the church, but He goes on to reveal something special about gathering together in unity of spirit in prayer. Jesus essentially said, "When just two believers agreed together in what they were asking for in prayer, their prayer would be granted to them." During Jesus' time, it was Jewish tradition that required at least 10 men to be present at the synagogue to hold public prayer. Here, Jesus promised to be present in the midst of an even smaller flock—of just two or three witnesses gathered in His name. Of course, all answers to prayer are contingent upon praying according to God's will. This insight was revealed to us by the Apostle John when he said, "And this is the confidence that we have in him, that, if we ask anything according to his will, he heareth us: and if we know that he hear us; whatsoever we ask, we know that we have the petitions that we desired (asked) of him" (1 John 5:14-15). But the major point is this—there is power in unity! God promises to be present when just two or three gather together in Jesus' name and agree in prayer!

I have experienced firsthand the power of gathering around the prayer chair in unity of spirit, and it has been a life-changing experience for me. I strongly believe that a spiritual synergy occurs as we gather around the prayer chair and begin to pray passionately in agreement over the same prayer requests. This corporate act of gathering around the chair in unity of spirit magnifies the power of our prayers. As our supercharged prayers are sent up, the presence of heaven falls down upon us, and almighty God joins us as we lift our prayers to heaven.

There are several Biblical examples of support for God answering prayers when people gather together in agreement as they ask Him to answer their prayers. One of those examples played out in the Old Testament book of Esther. Haman developed a hatred for Mordecai and plotted to kill all the Jews in order to eliminate Mordecai and his people. Mordecai turned to Queen Esther to help fool Haman's plan for genocide. When Mordecai went to encourage Esther to speak with King Ahasuerus about this evil plot, she told him that she had not been called to see the king for more than thirty days. Esther knew if she risked approaching the king without being called, it could mean certain death! Mordecai reminded her she would be dead either way if she didn't risk her life to save her people. In fact, Mordecai said, "...who knoweth whether thou art come to the kingdom for such a time as this" (Esther 4:14)? Wow, talk about pressure! In response, Esther called for united prayer and fasting and told Mordecai to, "Go gather together all the Jews that are present in Shushan, and fast ye for me, and neither eat nor drink three days, night or day: I also and my maidens will fast likewise; and so will I go into the king, which is not according to the law: and if I perish, I perish" (Esther 4:16). God heard their cries and answered their prayer of unity. Not only were the Jews saved, but the king actually sentenced Haman to be hanged on the gallows he had prepared for Mordecai. Praying in agreement really works!

In the New Testament, one of the greatest examples of the power of united prayer comes from the book of Acts. After Jesus ascended back into heaven after His death, burial, and resurrection, His close inner circle of believers gathered in the upper room in Jerusalem to pray. "They all continued with one accord (or mind) in prayer and supplication, with the women, and Mary the mother of Jesus, and with his brethren" (Acts 1:14). They were awaiting the promised Comforter Jesus spoke of in John 16:7. After ten days of united prayer, the Holy Spirit fell upon them in what came to be known as the Day of Pentecost, "And when the day of Pentecost was fully come, they were all with one accord (purpose or mind) in one place. And suddenly there came a sound from heaven as a rushing mighty wind, and it filled all the house where they were sitting" (Acts 2: 1-2). They began to miraculously testify of the glories of God in the native tongues of the Jewish pilgrims who gathered in Jerusalem from regions all over the world. The Apostle Peter then preached and over three thousand souls were saved that day. Wow, the power of prayer! It was no coincidence the New Testament Church was birthed in a prayer meeting! After all, the Prophet Isaiah clearly revealed that God had said,"...mine house shall be called a house of prayer for all people" (Isaiah 56:7).

There are many other Biblical examples such as the story of Jehoshaphat in 2 Chronicles chapter 20, or the story in Acts 4:23-31 where Apostles Peter and John prayed for boldness to spread the gospel, or the story in Acts 12:5 where the Apostle Peter was freed by an angel of the Lord. Biblical stories abound where God's people were saved, baptized, healed (physically, mentally, emotionally, and spiritually) and set free from their bondage of sin. In each case, it all started when God's people united together as one and began to agree together in prayer!

PRAYER AND FASTING

Prayer and fasting are two of our greatest spiritual weapons against Satan. The Word of God, our faith, and the name of Jesus are all weapons in our spiritual warfare against evil. Prayer and fasting are not just great spiritual disciplines to embrace our own personal spiritual growth and development; they are genuine spiritual weapons given to us by God for our battle against Satan.

The real purpose of fasting is to bring the body and soul into subjection, so while we are praying, we will be focused solely on God and His will for that person's life. Each of us possesses natural desires and appetites that are a part of our creation. These desires are to be satisfied in a proper manner according to God's Word, so the fulfillment of our desires and appetites will be for the glory of God. For example, we have an appetite for food, we have a natural appetite for beauty, we have an appetite for sex, all of which are to be satisfied within the bounds of God's commandments.

There are times, however, when God desires for us to set aside these natural desires and appetites to concentrate solely on spiritual matters. True fasting goes beyond skipping meals or denying ourselves food for a specified period of time. The Prophet Isaiah revealed God's preferred way of fasting to us when he said, "Is it such a fast that I have chosen? A day for a man to afflict his soul? Is it to bow down his head as a bulrush, and to spread sackcloth and ashes under him? Wilt thou call this a fast, and an acceptable day to the Lord? Is not this the fast that I have chosen? To lose the bands of wickedness, to undo the heavy burdens, and to let the oppressed go free, and that ye break every yoke? Is it not to deal (share) thy bread to the hungry, and that thou bring the poor that are (wandering) out to thy house? When thou seest the naked, that thou cover him; and that thou hide not thyself from thine own flesh" (Isaiah 58:5-7)? True fasting is a denial of all natural human appetites for a season, so we might concentrate solely on the Lord and what He wants to say or do for us.

There are times in our lives when we are desperate for God to hear our cries and He will place a desire in our heart to fast and pray. Jesus warned us these days would come when He said, "...this kind goeth not out but by prayer and fasting" (Matthew 17:21). Certain situations and problems simply cannot be resolved apart from fasting and prayer (2 Corinthians 10:4). When we require our hearts and minds to maintain an intense focus in prayer, it is time too fast! When you are truly called by God to fast and pray, you will have a greater desire to pray and be with the Lord than you will to eat, sleep, or do anything else.

Prayer can change things! We can impact our families, our churches, our communities, our nation, and our world through prayer. As we fast and pray, God will move! He will pour out His Spirit, in His ways and in His timing!

Chapter 5 What We Pray For?

Before we gather in corporate worship, one of the keys to experiencing a powerful prayer life is to prepare our hearts to come before God. We are blessed to be led by preachers who have learned how to be sensitive to the direction of the Holy Spirit and then move in the direction the Spirit wants to move. In the modern church, this is often not even an option, as most churches adhere to a tight schedule or timeline of events. They schedule a certain number of songs, short time for prayer and testimony, and then the preacher is usually given between twenty-five to thirty-five minutes to deliver a message and then there is a short invitation before leaving for lunch. Where is God in this type of schedule? Is He even a factor in this type of service? This is one of the keys to why we are able to unlock the power of God through the prayer chair! During our services, we might gather together, and the Spirit moves us towards a worship and testimony service that can last for several hours. The next week, the prayer burden might be heavy and we spend the entire service gathered around the prayer chair, praying for others. Thank God we are being led by Godly preachers who are sensitive to the Holy Spirit and care more about moving in the direction God wants them to move than they are about making sure they get to deliver their sermon or pass the collection plate. In order to experience a powerful and effective prayer life as a body of Christ, you must be led by the Holy Spirit and not a church committee's tight scheduling.

When we gather together in corporate worship, our prayers are often driven by prayer requests we receive from the body of Christ itself, as well as from others outside the church. As a church body, when we gather around the prayer chair, our prayers are almost always directed towards praying for others. Our prayers are diverse and cover many requests from all over the world. I would like to share with you some of the things we pray for as we gather around the prayer chair.

PRAYING FOR THE LOST

If all believers were completely honest, they would have to admit that a majority of their prayers are directed towards themselves rather than others. Only after praying for their own needs, would they admit their prayers are directed towards their families, followed by their friends and relatives. But God desires for us to pray for the lost specifically. The Apostle Paul was arguably one of the giants of the faith in the Bible. One reason he is held in such high regard was his love for the lost. He loved them so much that he prayed, "Brethren, my heart's desire and prayer to God for Israel is, that they might be saved" (Romans 10:1). As a part of the body of Christ, we need to view praying for the lost as a priority and spend time committed to this, just as the Apostle Paul did.

As we gather around the prayer chair to pray for others, we often become burdened for the lost. If we are praying for someone and unsure if they are a believer or not, we pray that God would save them if they are lost. When we pray, we call out their name just as the Apostle Paul did when he said, "...without ceasing I make mention of you always in my prayers" (Romans 1:9). We pray for God to open the eyes of the lost and reveal Himself to them in a way that only they can understand, and to help them realize their need for a Savior. When we are praying for someone we cannot reach or gain access to, we will ask Him to send a God-fearing preacher their way to share the gospel, love, and forgiveness of Jesus Christ.

Our prayers are never limited to praying for those who are within our area of influence. Most of the lost we pray for are those whom we have never met. We pray God would anoint missionaries to be able to share the gospel with the lost and that God would save them. We pray for our leaders to hear the gospel and realize their need for forgiveness and salvation as they lead our communities, our states, and our nation. Yes, we pray for all the lost on an ongoing basis.

So how do we pray for the lost? We pray for God to work in their hearts and open their spirits so they might be able to receive the truth of the gospel. We pray God would place a hedge of protection and spirit of peace around them so He can deal with their hearts. We pray God would put them under Holy Ghost conviction and bring them to true repentance and create a desire in them to be saved through the blood of Jesus Christ. Finally, we pray for God's blessings, guidance, protection and presence to be on those who surrender their lives to Him.

When we realize the lost are spiritually blind, hopeless, and facing eternity in hell without Christ, just as we once were, it should create a sense of urgency to pray for the lost.

PRAYING FOR OTHER BELIEVERS

Perhaps some of the most commonly spoken words in the modern Church today are, "I'll be praying for you." Just imagine the condition our Churches would be in if those empty promises were actually kept! We need and should covet each other's prayers. The most loving thing we can do for one another is to pray for each other. When adversity strikes, it is very comforting to know you are not alone, that your Christian family has your back and is willing to do anything to support you. Praying for other believers was a major part of the Apostle Paul's ministry. He provides great Biblical insight when he said, "Praying always with all prayer and supplication in the Spirit, and watching thereunto with all perseverance and supplication for all saints" (Ephesians 6:18). A healthy, functioning church should pray for one another. Prayer has the power to heal us, to strengthen us, to bond us. It has the power to unite the body of Christ as one!

In our church, we are always praying for one another as well as other believers who have requested prayer. Depending on their needs, we might pray for healing and restoration, wisdom, a hedge of protection, guidance, favor, etc. Whatever the need, we are to pray for other believers according to God's will!

PRAYING FOR FAMILY

In the modern church, much of the prayers you often hear consist of asking God to "Bless," "Be with," or "Watch over" a member of our family. These prayers lack the fervor and specificity I believe needed to move God through prayer. Our prayers should be much more focused than this! When we pray for our families, we should know for who, and specifically for what, we are praying for. General prayers will result in general answers. We will be able to praise God more, giving Him all the glory when we pray specifically for our loved ones.

Praying specifically for our families is something we have been taught to do by our pastors and it has helped us unlock the power of prayer. There is nothing more amazing than having the opportunity to gather around the prayer chair with other brothers to cry out to God on behalf of their loved ones. While we do pray for all our loved ones, including our mothers, fathers, siblings, aunts, uncles, and cousins, we spend a majority of our time praying for our spouses and our children. I have witnessed broken men crying out to God for their spouses and then watched as God lovingly restored their marriage despite their circumstances. All married Christians should pray for their spouse. In fact, we should pray, "Father, I ask you to help me love my wife just as Christ loved the church and gave Himself for it" (Ephesians 5:25). We should pray, "That God would guide our lives in an understanding way that we might honor our wives so that our prayers will not be hindered" (1 Peter 3:7). We should also pray for God's protection over our marriages as well. It still holds true, a couple that prays together, stays together. Not only should we pray for our spouses, but we should also desire to pray with them.

We should also pray for our children, and this is a great prayer burden in our church. Most don't realize that children of prisoners are seven times more likely than other children to become incarcerated themselves prior to age 25. This is an enormous burden all incarcerated parents carry as a collateral consequence of their incarceration. There is nothing more disheartening than watching a father on his knees before the altar of God crying out for Him to save and protect their children. Statistically, once the cycle of multigenerational incarceration takes root, it will perpetuate itself unless a broken father is willing to humble himself before the throne of grace, asking God to break the cycle of multigenerational incarceration.

When praying for our children we should also pray and claim specific verses in scripture that applies to areas such as salvation (Acts 3:19), spiritual growth and maturity (1 Peter 3:18), the filling of the Holy Spirit (Luke 11:13), moral purity (2 Timothy 2:22), protection, direction and guidance (Psalm 32:8), honoring their parents and/or guardian (Ephesians 6:1-3), and most importantly to guide them in the choice of their friends (Proverbs 18:24). Satan is heavily invested in causing your children confusion, leading them to doubt their self-worth and identity. Your role as a parent is to stand in the gap for your children, interceding on their behalf before the throne of grace. Offering up these verses for your children will have an eternal impact on their lives as well as your grandchildren (Isaiah 59:21).

We also pray for others in our families when they stand in need of prayer, but mostly we pray for our marriages and our children. If we are obedient in our daily walk with God, the Holy Spirit will steadily unlock His word so we can pray for our families and future generations according to His perfect will for their lives. It's time to stop praying generic prayers for those we love and care about the most, and instead start praying deliberately for them. God will honor this just as He honors our prayers as we intercede on their behalf in the prayer chair.

PRAYING FOR AUTHORITIES

Every action or decision made by someone in authority creates a significant impact on those within their sphere of influence. Since the leadership of those in authority can have such a powerful impact on our lives, the Bible commands us to pray for those in authority over us. In fact, 1 Timothy 2:1-2 says, "I exhort therefore, that, first of all, supplications, prayers, intercessions, and giving of thanks, be made for all men; for Kings, and for all that are in authority; that we may lead a quiet a peaceable life in all godliness and honesty." We would be wise to pray for those in authority who have so much influence over our lives.

You would think the last thing anyone who is incarcerated would want to do is pray for those in authority over them, but as a thriving, mature body of Christ, this is exactly what we spend a significant amount of time doing in the prayer chair. But how, and why, would prisoners pray for those who might treat us harshly or even as mere chattel instead of human beings with dignity? The answer to this question lies in Romans 13:1-2, when the Apostle Paul warned us to, "Let every soul be subject unto higher (governing) powers (authorities). For there is no power (authority) but of God; the powers (authorities) that be are ordained (appointed by) of God. Whosoever therefore resisteth the power (authority) of God: resisteth the ordinance of God; and they that resist shall receive to themselves damnation (judgment)." God's warning could not be more clear, all authority on earth is ordained by Him, and anyone who disobeys their authority is disobeying God Himself and will suffer judgment. This command to honor authority is often even more difficult for the incarcerated, considering a unique challenge many of them are facing. According to the America First Policy Institute, 70 percent of incarcerated individuals are a product of a broken home and never had a father present in their lives. When a father is absent in the lives of their children, it often sows a spirit of distrust for authority which consumes their lives. This seed of distrust for authority is the polar opposite of how God commands all believers to view authority, so when we gather around the prayer chair to pray for those in authority over us, we are experiencing an amazing act of grace and healing in our own lives. It takes an enormous amount of trust in the Lord to be able to overcome our natural tendency to resist authority over us.

As we gather around the prayer chair, we often pray for those in authority as well as their families and loved ones. We pray for their salvation, for God to guide them according to His will, for God to enhance their ability to lead and govern over our lives, for their commitment to the highest moral standards, in both their private and professional lives. While we pray for them, it is also important for us to realize that, although each of us answers to someone higher than ourselves—parents, law enforcement, public officials, supervisors, prison administration—most of us also represent some kind of authority over others as well: children, employees, students, anyone who looks to us for guidance, direction, and instruction. So the Biblical command to pray for those in authority equally applies to these relationships as well; we must take our responsibilities very seriously and perform them with great care and honor God demands of us, knowing we will one day give an account for how we treat others.

When we pray for those in authority over us, we are to pray upward in support of those who lead us, as well as downward towards those under our authority and care. When we do this, we are praying according to the will of God and in the best interest of everyone within our sphere of influence.

PRAYING FOR LABORERES IN THE HARVEST

We are living in the midst of a broken and fallen world and God wants us to open our eyes and realize the multitudes are hurting, empty, and hopelessly wandering through life searching for purpose and meaning, just like a sheep without a shepherd. The modern church has forgotten what Jesus taught us when He saw the multitudes: "He was moved with compassion on them, because they fainted (were weary), and were scattered abroad, as sheep having no shepherd. Then saith He unto His disciples, the harvest truly is plenteous, but the laborers are few; pray ye therefore the Lord of the harvest, that He will send forth laborers into His harvest" (Matthew 9: 36-38). Jesus was moved with deep compassion for the lost, and we should be as well. All believers should be praying for God to send more laborers into His harvest field of souls. We desperately need more Godly people serving in the ministries across the globe to help serve in our broken world.

Just consider how much of an impact one person who is completely sold out and totally surrendered to God can have on the world. If they are truly living a spirit-filled life for God and spreading the gospel, they will radically impact marriages, families, churches, businesses, and their communities. Just think about it, the Old Testament books of Ezra, Nehemiah, and Esther all show how one person who is completely surrendered and sold out to God can impact and transform an entire nation. Praying God would raise up more spirit-filled servants is a spiritual bomb-dropping prayer that can transform our fallen world!

Too often, the modern church becomes preoccupied with the comforts of this world and gets obsessed with praying for their own personal needs, while forgetting the spiritual tragedy of a lost and fallen world that is playing out before our very eyes. While we oftentimes think the task of bearing the burden of praying for our fallen generation seems too great or overwhelming, we are to remind ourselves, "...with God, all things are possible" (Matthew 19:26). Every believer is called to be a laborer in God's harvest field. Jesus commands us to pray specifically for laborers in the ministry—not just for general blessings, but with a strategic passion and focused precision for their most urgent needs. Whether you are a mighty prayer warrior, or taking an active part in a ministry, we all have a role to play in God's harvest field.

Our church carries a great burden to pray for laborers of the harvest. As we gather around the prayer chair, we often pray specifically for our pastor as well as pastors across the world. All pastors need an army of mighty prayer warriors in their corner to lift them up before the throne of grace on a daily basis. Their work is eternal, and it's draining and demanding. The responsibilities placed on them are often overwhelming and endless. Not only are they fighting a spiritual battle against the devil over the souls of the flock, but they must also fulfill their Biblical obligations as a husband, father, and leader in their local community. If this enormous burden were not enough, when Satan cannot defeat a man of God directly, he will attack our pastors through their marriages, their children, and their families. Satan knows a successful attack on a pastor's home is a successful attack on the church itself. That's why he wants to attack their homes, their health, and their Godly ministries. While much of a pastor's service is visible, many of their responsibilities remain private—laboring in study in preparation for service, providing spiritual counsel, visiting the sick and shut in, and mediating a never-ending stream of conflict within the church. They carry this enormous burden, amid constant murmuring opposition, often from within the church itself. This causes our pastors to grow weary and discouraged beneath the burden of eternal work. We must not forget, they too are tempted by the same sins and temptations as we are. That's why pastors across the globe desperately need our prayers. If you want a better pastor, quit complaining and pray for the one God has already given you!

When we gather around the prayer chair, we often pray for God to place His hedge of protection around our pastor's heart, his marriage, his children, and his home. We pray God would anoint him with the fire and the power of the Holy Spirit to unapologetically deliver the message of the gospel to our church. We pray he would be sensitive to the guidance and direction of the Holy Spirit, allowing him to be led in the direction God wants us to travel. We pray God would allow him to boldly put God and His kingdom first before anyone or anything else. We pray God would use our pastor to deliver the life-changing gospel to the lost and remove their spiritual blindness so they might be drawn unto Him and saved. Remember, prayer has the power to change the trajectory of our world!

Not only do we pray for our pastors, but we also pray for missionaries across the world as well. We often forget these missionaries have uprooted their families and relocated them across the globe in often dangerous locations to serve others while sharing the gospel. At home, our missionaries are feeding and clothing the poor, rescuing abused and battered women and children, rescuing sexually exploited women, and rescuing young pregnant women from the destructive impact of abortion. While across the globe, they are helping to introduce new agricultural concepts to under-developed countries, building churches and training pastors, building hospitals, building orphanages, rescuing victims of sexual slavery, or even helping to establish life-saving infrastructure such as water wells and sewer systems. The tasks of our missionaries are endless. As we pray for them, it magnifies the gospel in cultures across the globe, so the lost might experience the love of Christ through them and be directed toward our Lord and Savior Jesus Christ.

THERE'S SOMETHING ABOUT THAT CHAIR!

In our modern churches across America, the message of Jesus Christ seems to be common; we cannot be lulled into complacency, forgetting all the other nations across the globe where the message of the gospel remains unknown. If we cannot do anything else, we can pray for the laborers of the harvest! If you are not currently praying for your pastor, other pastors around the world, or our brave missionaries, I would encourage you to join us as we impact the world through prayer.

PRAYER FOR CHURCHES AND REVIVAL

The modern church has surrendered its Biblical responsibilities to our governments. As a result, the church has caved to the sinful liberalism and hopelessness that has gripped our nation and our world. The church has now succumbed to the apathy, fear, and belief that the complex social problems we now face are so overwhelming nothing can be done about it. They have become weary and disinterested, making little to no impact for the kingdom of Christ in their families, their neighborhoods, their communities, much less our nation or the rest of the world. Believers have been lulled into complacency where they have begun to tolerate their own sins, consumed by their own selfish ambitions, content with their lifeless religion, while millions are hopelessly lost and dying without Jesus.

The church has forsaken its first love and stands in need of a spiritual awakening across our nation and our world. There is no reason why we can't see God's Spirit poured out on our churches like in days past. The only way to change the trajectory of our churches, our local communities, our nation, and our world is a good old Holy Ghost revival. In order for this to occur, revival must begin at the house of God through the hearts of all believers. It will take believers who become desperate for God, desiring for Him to revive their families and restore broken lives. I have personally experienced revival in our prison around the same time the prayer chair was conceptualized. I can remember the spirit of God becoming so profound that it felt like a thick fog had settled throughout the church and you could literally feel the presence of an almighty God as He moved across the sanctuary. The sweet embrace of the Holy Spirit is so powerful it will leave you speechless, humbled, and in tears. I often long for those times to return again! There is nothing more spiritually rewarding than getting your own heart right before God and witnessing droves of lost people coming to salvation through Jesus Christ, drawing more and more people each and every day. Watching as broken men jump up in the middle of a service shouting, "Preacher, I'm lost and I need to get saved. I can't wait any longer!" Watching as the church erupts in jubilation and applause over one lost person coming to Christ! Watching as God miraculously breaks the bondage of sin and delivers His broken people from a life of addiction to drugs, alcohol, depression, pornography, gambling, abuse, violence, anger, bitterness, self-destruction, made completely free, replacing it with a pure life of spiritual freedom. Watching as racial tensions are shattered and replaced by God's love, forgiveness, understanding, and respect. Watching as bitter rivals from opposing gangs become brothers in Christ, laying down their colors to become servants of the most high God instead of the devil. Watching as broken families and estranged love ones are lovingly restored. Watching as once social castaways become the solution to solving the crime problems in their communities instead of helping to perpetuate it. Watching as our churches are filled to overflowing by a unified body of Christ experiencing a spiritual hunger for revival that will transform our families, our churches, our communities, our nation, and our world. Once you have experienced a revival like this, you will always long for the sweet embrace of the Holy Spirit to return you to the point of revival.

There's no reason why our modern churches can't experience a revival like I once did and personally witness all these things—and much more. Remember, God is able to do, "...exceedingly abundantly above all we can ask or think, according to the power that worketh in us" (Ephesians 3:20). This same power, "That worketh in us," is the same power that raised Christ from the dead (Romans 8:11)! Imagine what we could experience if we activated this power within us, instead of continuing to allow it to lie dormant, slowly withering away.

While preparing our own hearts for revival, all believers should pray specific scriptures in faith: "That righteousness will exalt (our) Nation, and that sin will no longer be a reproach to (our) people" (Proverbs 14:34); "That God will revive His work in our Nation in the midst of the years, and in wrath He will remember mercy" (Habakkuk 3:2); "That God will revive His people again that they might rejoice in Him" (Psalms 85:6); "That God's people will repent and return to Him that their sins might be wiped away, that a time of refreshing might come to them from the presence of the Lord" (Acts 3:19); and, "The glory of the Lord will fill the house of the Lord" (2 Chronicles 7:1).

If all believers would pray fervently and faithfully for a spiritual awakening, God would hear the cries of His church, and according to His perfect timing, would send an outpouring of His Holy Spirit upon His church that would literally shake the foundation of our Nation for Jesus Christ! The secret is united, repentant, humble, and persistent prayer from all believers! Join us as we pray for revival in our lives, our families, our churches, our communities, our nation, and our world.

Chapter 6 Answered Prayers!

I have personally witnessed as God has answered hundreds of prayers through the prayer chair over the past 15 years. Most of these answers to prayers are deeply personal to me because they either involve one of my loved ones or a close brother or sister in Christ that I deeply care about. This is why I feel compelled to share some of the stories of the most extraordinary answers to our prayers. Only the first names of many of the participants have been used in order to preserve their privacy. I pray these stories will inspire you to start your own prayer chair!

One of our dear brothers in Christ, Matthew Patterson, wrote a poem which powerfully depicts the great emphasis our church places on prayer. This poem was given to him by inspiration of the Holy Spirit as a result of Brother Ken Avery asking one of our prayer warriors to, "Take us to the throne of grace," as we gathered around the prayer chair one evening. He drew inspiration from Hebrews 4:16, which declares, "Let us therefore come boldly unto the throne of grace, that we may obtain mercy, and find grace to help in time of need." I felt compelled to share it with you because I am certain it will encourage you to boldly come before the throne of grace anytime you, a loved one, or someone you care about, have a need only God can provide.

"TAKE US TO THE THRONE"©
Written By: Matthew Patterson

I stood up in church one night to share my heart,
A storm was raging that threatened to tear me apart.
The pain I felt was so real and so deep,
It was hard to talk when I wanted to weep.

My ship was drifting, and the enemy told me I was alone,
Then one brother turned to another and said, "Take us to the
throne."

As the brothers gathered round me, I felt such relief,
For these were prayer warriors, mighty in belief.
They had been through many battles and had seen what prayer could
do,
And now they were praying for God to bring me through.
These men claimed the blood of Jesus, which did for sin atone,
They prayed with holy boldness when they took me to the throne.

You may be fighting a battle you cannot seem to win,
Satan may be bringing up your past when you were last in sin.
You may feel that all is hopeless and there's nothing you can do,
It may seem the nights too dark and you are all but through.
You may have a burden as heavy as a thousand pound stone,
But you will see the victory when you're taken to the throne!

GOD IS MORE POWERFUL THAN GANGS

One sweltering evening, we gathered together for our weekly Friday night service. After a few songs of worship, Brother Ken Avery asked, "If there was anyone who wanted to stand up and testify before the Church?" After a brief moment, a man name Gerald stood up and began to share a story about his young son. From the moment he began to talk, you could tell he was broken and hurting. Gerald shared with everyone that, "His young son was being heavily recruited by a notorious street gang in his town and it was causing an enormous amount of friction in his home." Not only was Gerald concerned for the safety of his son and his family, but he was broken because he was bearing the burden of guilt for not being present in the home to raise his young son. The consequences of his actions were playing out before his very eyes, and he was desperate to save his young son.

A few days prior, a huge fight occurred between Gerald's young son and his mother. The fight became so bad Gerald's son chose to leave home and join and live with the gang. Broken and despondent, Gerald was desperate before God. Brother Ken Avery quickly sensed the need of the moment and asked, "If we could pray for his son?" The prayer chair was placed at the front of the church and Gerald almost ran to jump in it! The church gathered around Brother Gerald, and we began to pray for his son. Heaven fell down in that little chapel on this night as the power of God overflowed our hearts. As we finished praying, there wasn't a dry eye in the house, and everyone gave Brother Gerald a hug and a word of encouragement. We excitedly awaited next week's service to hear how God would answer our prayers.

When the next Friday night service arrived, Brother Gerald was eager to stand up and testify about the goodness and mercy of God. Brother Gerald reported that, "Through a series of miraculous events, his son had quit the gang and returned home to live safely with his mother." The entire church erupted in praise as God had lovingly restored Gerald's son back to his home safely without any harm or trouble. We serve a big God who hears the cries of His children!

GOD CARES FOR OUR CHILDREN

I have often witnessed as broken and dejected fathers kneel at the altar of God crying out in desperation for their children. This Friday night's service was no different. One of our dear members, Brother Rick, was broken and hurting from the time he entered through the door. As he bravely tried to stand up and share his heart with the brethren, he broke down in tears. Like most incarcerated fathers, they feel a deep sense of contrition for deserting their children, often leaving them confused and feeling hopelessly abandoned. Brother Rick was no different. He had recently received news from the State of Tennessee that they were petitioning the court to terminate his parental rights and put his child up for adoption. The thought of losing the child you helped conceive and raise is definitely heartbreaking and more than most can bear. Brother Rick was adamant about not wanting to lose his only child to adoption. Brother Ken Avery sensed the need and asked Brother Rick to come and sit in the prayer chair. As we gathered around with heavy hearts, you could sense the desperation of the moment. We prayed fervently that God would step in to help Brother Rick's situation and keep his young son safe and in a Christian home.

Unfortunately, Brother Rick's situation is a common one, and any time a person is sentenced to more than 10 years in a prison in Tennessee, they can have their parental rights terminated by a court of law.

Within a few weeks, Brother Rick was contacted by the social worker assigned to his son's case. Amazingly, the social worker told Brother Rick that a Christian family in Florida wanted to adopt his young son and they wanted Brother Rick to remain present is his son's life. This is almost unheard of in the adoption industry, and the family also wanted to speak with Brother Rick as soon as possible. Once again, God had heard our cries and had placed Brother Rick's son in a loving Christian home. Although Brother Rick remains incarcerated, he has a close, loving relationship with his son and his newly adopted family. God is still in the miracle business!

GOD: THE GREAT PHYSICIAN

Early on Thursday morning, I was called to the Chaplain's office and told, "My mother was in ICU and I needed to call home immediately." In fact, he said, "He would call for me right now." I was able to get into contact with my stepfather and he told me, "My mother was in critical condition and he wasn't sure if she was going to make it." The news was devastating, and it crushed me! My stepfather told me, "She was asking for me to come visit her before she died." He told me, "She had been diagnosed with a blood clot on her right kidney but they were unsure how to treat it because it was such a rare condition." To compound the problem, she waited almost two weeks to see a doctor, which allowed a serious sepsis infection to set up in her body. My mother was fighting for her life! There is no worse feeling that being incarcerated and powerless to do anything about a situation, or to be there to handle things as a man should. But I was not as powerless as one might think; I immediately went back to my housing unit and hit my knees to pray for my mother. Later that afternoon, I was able to speak with her, but I could sense the pain and desperation in her voice. She told me, "If I didn't hurry up and come to visit her, she was going to die of a broken heart." Hearing her say this overwhelmed me! I prayed throughout the night, hoping she would be able to make it until I could get to the prayer chair Friday night.

I was able to speak with her again Friday afternoon and the news was dire. My mother was writhing in so much pain she was now absolutely certain she was dying. While we were talking, she would spontaneously scream out in pain, desperate for relief that never came. Imagine being on the other end of a telephone speaking to your mother, having to listen to her screaming out in pain and agony, powerless to say or do anything to make her better. I all but ran to church Friday night and immediately pulled Brother Ken Avery to the side to tell him what was going on. The service had no more begun when Brother Avery pulled a chair to the front of the church and told them, "We had an urgent need to pray over my mother." As I told the church what was going on, it was all I could do to hold it together. There is no greater comfort for me than to be surrounded by an army of mighty prayer warriors to lift me up in a moment of desperation before the throne of grace, so I might obtain mercy in a time of need. As we began to pray, you could sense the presence of the Holy Spirit moving throughout the Church. There is nothing more powerful than having over sixty of my brothers in Christ gathered around the prayer chair, crying out in unity for the health of my precious mother.

Later that evening after the service, I was able to get in touch with my mother and miraculously, the intense pain she was experiencing was gone and she was now resting comfortably. Within a week, the doctors had figured out how to treat the blood clot. Her kidney function had returned from almost nonfunctioning to completely normal, the sepsis infection had disappeared, and she was trending in the right direction.

At the next Friday night's service, I could not wait to share the news with the church. After taking a victory lap around the church, we praised the Lord for the Great Physician hearing our cries once again. It is important to share with the church when another victory for the mighty prayer warriors has been won. It is also important to give all the praise and glory to God for any answer to prayer. So, thank you Lord for healing my mother!

GOD WORKS MIRACLES THROUGH THE CHURCH

On January 12, 2010, at 4:53 p.m., one of the worst natural disasters in Haiti's history occurred as a magnitude 7 earthquake struck the tiny island. It was the most powerful earthquake to strike Haiti in more than two hundred years. It killed over 316,000 people and forced more than a million people from their homes. Many of the Haitian people went missing. The disaster added to the troubles of one of the most densely populated and least developed countries in the Western Hemisphere.

The Haiti earthquake devastated the infrastructure of the already struggling country. Most of the homes, schools, hospitals, and government buildings collapsed due to poor structural design. Search and rescue teams from around the world were quickly deployed to search for and help the earthquake survivors. However, Haiti's main airport was damaged, making it almost impossible to deliver emergency supplies, food, water, and medical equipment to the devastated country. Worldwide media coverage ensured the devastating impact of the earthquake was on full display for the entire world to see.

One of our brothers in Christ, Benoit, was from the Nation of Haiti and the news of the earthquake crushed him. He had great concern for the safety of his family and for the survivors of the earthquake. The mighty prayer warriors quickly sprang into action as we gathered around the prayer chair to pray for his family and the Nation of Haiti. The Lord met with us that night and heard our cries, and within a few weeks, we learned that everyone in Benoit's family was safe.

God also taught us something very important about prayer that fateful day that changed the trajectory of our prayer lives. It is always important to remember when you are praying in faith, you must be prepared to step in and fulfill a need if God calls you to do so. Within days of the earthquake, we heard of the devastating impact the earthquake had on the children of Haiti. We heard that many of the children had been trapped in the rubble of collapsed buildings and suffered serious injuries which required doctors to amputate their limbs. Now many of these children were hopelessly laying in makeshift hospital tents with no way to maneuver around without their limbs. All children hold a special place in our church's heart, so hearing news about these children really tugged at our heart strings. Within a few days of our prayer, we were told of a ministry that had established the ability to fly in and out of Haiti. They were about to partner with another organization who was planning to fly in wheelchairs for children impacted by the earthquake. A great burden developed as we continued to pray for the Haitian people. This is when God taught us when we pray we must be prepared to step in to fulfill a need if God calls you to do so. The prayer burden developed to raise money to purchase wheelchairs for the impacted children of Haiti. Our Chaplain at the time, Pastor Larry Glenn, was able to establish contact quickly with the organization planning to send the wheelchairs to Haiti, as well as obtain permission from our warden to raise money for the purchase of the wheelchairs. The plan was to send the money to the organization that would then purchase and fly the wheelchairs to Haiti. The problem was, the specialized wheelchairs for children cost $195 each and most of the mighty prayer warriors only made between .17 to .50 cents an hour from their prison jobs. Most of these men barely make $19.00 per month if they don't have any of it taken for fines or court costs. How would these unlikely men possibly be able to make an impact by purchasing these expensive wheelchairs for the Haitian children? We had to remind ourselves, "...with God, all things are possible" (Matthew 19:26)! The mighty prayer warriors began to gather to fight the battle around the prayer chair, and God gave them a vision and a plan to accomplish the task at hand. Within a week, we had raised enough money to purchase 19 wheelchairs to send to the Haitian children. A miracle had fallen down from heaven in response to the cry of His mighty prayer warriors!

We learned two very important lessons. First, when God gives the vision, He will provide the provision to accomplish His will; and, second, God will give through you what He will not give to you! It was a spiritually rewarding experience to witness God use the most unlikely of men to impact the world!

GOD CAN FLY?

We often pray for our missionaries across the globe. Our church has adopted several of these missionaries as our own. One missionary, John Schrader, and his entire family, hold a special place in our hearts. John is the father of 14 children and God put a burden on his heart to uproot his entire family and relocate them to Zambia, Africa, to start a ministry. When they arrived, John set up his ministry right next door to a Muslim mosque, setting the stage for an epic battle of spiritual warfare. Of course, we all know who will win that battle!

After a few months, John came to the realization he needed a plane so he could easily transport his family and move supplies to the remote location where his ministry was located. He asked the mighty prayer warriors to pray God would open a door to allow him to find a plane. When we received word the Schrader family had a need, we quickly gathered around the prayer chair to cry out on their behalf. The Spirit of God moved throughout the church as we prayed.

Within a few weeks, Brother Ken Avery received word from John that a gentleman had made contact with him to tell him, "God told me you needed a plane, and He wanted me to give the one I have to you!" He then asked in jest, "You do need a plane don't you?" When the church heard this, we broke out in praise and jubilation that God had heard our cry and provided a plane for the Schrader family. We continued to pray over the Schrader family and the plane, and within a month, the plane was shipped to Zambia, Africa, where God is still piloting that beautiful old plane.

NOTHING IS TOO HARD FOR GOD!

One evening, at our weekly Friday service, one of our dear brothers in Christ, James, came through the door and I could immediately tell something was wrong. I have known James for the entirety of my more than 25 years of incarceration. He was one of the Christian Brothers who took me under their wing when I first arrived to prison; keeping me from falling in with the wrong crowd or getting into trouble. As you can imagine, we have developed a very strong bond and friendship over the years, which is rare in prison. But as my brother hurt, so did I.

As the service began, James stood up and began to ask us to pray for his sister, which he affectionately calls, "Sis." She had been riding a horse across the yard one afternoon when she decided to see how the horse reacted when they doubled. This simply means having two riders on the horse's back at the same time. She rode up to the porch and her daughter hopped on to the horse with her. As they were riding across the yard, her daughter dug her heels into the horse's hocks and it caused the horse to become startled and it starting bucking. As it reared up on its hind legs, the 1,400 pound quarter horse threw both of them off, but Sis held on to the reins. As the horse continued to buck, it slung Sis around on a freshly cut stump crushing her foot! She was rushed to a little country hospital in Kentucky, and after they x-rayed her foot, they immediately determined they did not have the medical expertise to handle this type of injury and transferred her to a bigger hospital. At the next hospital, the doctors told Sis her foot was crushed so badly it could not be salvaged and she will probably need to have it amputated. She was then transferred to a third hospital where the doctors told her all they could do was amputate her foot. Everyone in the family was devastated and James was broken and desperately seeking God to save his Sis's foot!

As we gathered around the prayer chair to pray for Sis, there was a sense of urgency because we knew it was going to take a miracle from the Great

Physician to save Sis's foot. But we serve a mighty God and we know, "...with God, all things are possible" (Matthew 19:26)! As we prayed, the Spirit of God moved throughout the church like a rushing wind. We asked God to save Sis's foot and to bless the doctors with the wisdom they needed to know how to take care of her and fix her foot. We cried out with a fervency and vigor that would probably scare most church folk. We called down heaven that night and we knew Sis was in the capable hands of an almighty God!

As Sis was lying in a hospital bed worrying whether she was going to be able to keep her foot, God orchestrated a chance meeting between her and a nurse that had once worked for a foot specialist in Hendersonville, Tennessee. She said, "If anyone can fix that foot, it would be him," and immediately gave the local doctors the name of the specialist. The next day, Sis was transferred from Kentucky to a hospital in Hendersonville, Tennessee, where the foot specialist was able to save her foot. After many months of rehabilitation, Sis's life has returned to normal, and she still rides horses and praises God for saving her foot!

DRUG SMUGGLERS TO BIBLE SMUGGLERS

Our thriving church is constantly praying for many of the missionaries across the world. One missionary in particular, Brother Brian Fox, is one of those missionaries. Brother Fox has shared many of the stories of how he has been trying to help the people of Bolivia and share the gospel with them. One of his desires was to provide some Bibles to the incarcerated in Bolivia. The problem with this is Bolivia was being run by an indigenous dictatorship that prohibited Bibles from being brought into the country. When Brother Brian Fox contacted Brother Ken Avery, he asked, "If the mighty prayer warriors would pray that he would be able to figure out a way to get the Bibles into Bolivia?"

As we gathered around the prayer chair, we were driven to fervency by the injustice of prohibiting the Word of God from being allowed in Bolivia. Unfortunately, the modern church often takes for granted the freedoms we have here in America, and fails to realize that many of the other countries around the world lack the basic resources and freedoms we share. As we prayed, the Spirit of God fell throughout our church. We prayed God would open the door of Bolivia to allow us to get the gospel into the prisons and the rest of the Nation.

Within a few weeks, the opportunity arose for us to purchase copies of some booklets that contained the Gospel of John and the Book of Romans in it. A collection was taken up by our congregation and over 1,500 booklets were purchased. Next, God opened a door to allow us to have someone smuggle the booklets into Bolivia and deliver them to the prisoners of Bolivia. Imagine that, God miraculously transformed drug smugglers into Bible smugglers! Instead of destroying life, they were now giving it by sharing the gospel of Jesus Christ! Oh, what a mighty God we serve that is still in the business of transforming the hearts of men!

A GOD OF SECOND CHANCES

It was a typical sweltering, muggy Friday night service, or so we thought. When we arrived, you could tell there was a heavy burden on the hearts of many of the men present. After some time of praise and worship, Brother Ken Avery asked, "If anyone had anything on their heart, they wanted to share with the church." One of my dear brothers in Christ, Rodney, stood up, and immediately you could tell he was bearing a heavy burden on his heart. Broken and despondent, he shared that, "His young son, still a juvenile, had been arrested and was facing over 50 years in prison." While the details remained unknown at the time, what we did know was we needed God to move on this situation.

We gathered around Brother Rodney to pray for his son. As we began to pray, the Holy Spirit moved throughout the Church like a whirlwind and you could sense the presence of an almighty God. We prayed that God would place a hedge of protection around Rodney's son and that God would send a Bible-believing preacher by his way to share the gospel of Jesus Christ with him. We prayed God would use his circumstances to save him for the glory of God and turn his life around.

After more than three months, Rodney's son was scheduled to have a court appearance. Everyone eagerly awaited news from Brother Rodney when we returned to church on Friday. When I first laid eyes on Brother Rodney, you could sense a joy and glow about him that had escaped his grasp for many months. I could immediately tell God had done it again! As soon as we arrived and the service began, Brother Rodney jumped up and shared with us about the glory and goodness of God. He shared, "When his son went to court, the judge had dismissed all the charges against him and let his son go." The church erupted in applause and jubilation as we shouted to the Lord in praise and adoration, thanking Him for hearing our cries. We later learned that a woman who witnessed the crime came forward and told the judge that Rodney's son had nothing to do with it! Not only had God freed Rodney's son, but during his time of incarceration, he had come in contact with a Bible-believing preacher and God miraculously saved his son! God is truly and lawyer that has never lost a case!

NO PROBLEM IS TOO BIG FOR GOD

One of our Dear Pastors from the Calvary Baptist Prison Ministry is Brother Mark Green. He is an old fiery southern preacher whose entire family has a big heart for God. Pastor Green would often bring his son Ryan and his daughter Christian to praise and worship with us at church. Both of his children are talented musicians. His son Ryan can play the guitar and sing, while his daughter Christian can play the violin and sing with a voice of an angel.

Brother Mark came to service one Friday night, and we asked how his family was doing. As he began to break down and cry, you could sense the heavy burden he was carrying. He shared that, "His daughter Christian was suffering from a debilitating Crohn's disease that was causing his precious daughter to waste away." She had lost much of her weight and there was no sign things would get better. The treatment she needed was not covered by any insurance, so they were at a loss of what to do.

We quickly invited Brother Mark to come and sit in the prayer chair as we gathered around him. We ensured him we knew of a Great Physician that could heal our dear sister in Christ. As we prayed, the Spirit of God moved throughout the Church and you could sense the presence of an almighty God. We prayed God would move on Christian's situation and get her the help she needed, and to heal her by the authority of the Lord Jesus Christ! We prayed God would bless the hands and the minds of the doctors who are treating her and lift her up for the glory of God! We knew God would hear the cries of His mighty prayer warriors.

A few short weeks later, Brother Mark returned to one of our regular Friday night services. We again asked how his family was doing, but this time Brother Mark had a bliss and cheerfulness about him that was absent the last time he visited. He began to share that, "A few days after we prayed they were contacted by Vanderbilt Hospital in Nashville, Tennessee, one of the best research hospitals in the world, asking if Christian would be interested in participating in a new experimental Crohn's disease treatment." After having a short Holy Ghost fit thanking the Lord for answering our prayers, they quickly said, "Yes!" The treatment began almost immediately, and the results were dramatic! Brother Mark was elated with tears of joy that he had his precious daughter back!

Christian has now moved to Australia and married the love of her life. She has access to medical care for the Crohn's disease that is not currently authorized in America and she is doing well serving the Lord.

OUR FATHER IN HEAVEN

We are constantly praying for other pastors across the country and every year Brother Ken Avery travels to Louisiana to preach at some of their churches. One of those preachers is Pastor Keary Jordan of Fort Hope Baptist Church. In the general area of his church there was a little old run down trailer missing its doors, windows, and most of its floors. Even though this small trailer was uninhabitable, it was home for a young lady named Marylen. She constantly had to worry about the opossums, raccoons, snakes and a host of other critters crawling into her home. She was living in the midst of a dreadful, dire situation. After a time, Marylen moved into a nearby trailer with even worse living conditions, having no running water or electricity. Imagine having to live in these destitute conditions while trying to survive, attend school, and grow into a young lady all alone.

When we heard the story of Marylen, the mighty prayer warriors in our church quickly developed a prayer burden for this precious young lady. As we gathered around the prayer chair to pray for her, the Holy Spirit moved throughout the church and you could sense the presence of God. We prayed God would place His hedge of protection and spirit of peace over this young lady and bless her according to His will for her life. We prayed if she was lost that God would reveal Himself to her in a manner only she can understand, and draw her unto Himself and save this precious young lady. We reminded God of His promise, "When my father and my mother forsake me, then the Lord will take (take care of me) me up" (Psalm 27:10), and asked for Him to step in and take care of Marylen in the absence of her parents.

It wasn't long before we received our answer to prayer. Through Fort Hope's outreach ministry, the church began to pick Marylen up on a bus and bring her to the church. As she began to attend church, many in the church began to take notice of her. Their hearts began to yearn for the plight of her living conditions. The church began to start checking in on her living conditions and stepped up as a New Testament church and took care of her needs. A dear sister in the church began to go pick Marylen up each Wednesday and take her to her home to shower and wash her clothes. Before long, the dear sister invited Marylen to move in with her so she could experience a stable home and provide for her needs. Over time, the dear sister was married and God orchestrated the situation where she moved out and Marylen was able to take over the home. The Lord moved mightily in Marylen's life and she was miraculously saved by the grace of God.

Today, Marylen is happily married to Pastor Keary Jordan's son and they are both serving the Lord. Her husband often shares with Brother Ken Avery how people often approach him, making comments about how much he has helped Marylen. Surprisingly, he is quick to tell everyone that it is Marylen who has helped him and not him that has helped her. What an amazing God we serve!

GOD'S NOT DONE YET

It was a typical Friday night service, but I could tell there was something wrong with one of my dear Brother's in Christ James. As long as I can remember, his mother would visit him religiously every other week. For the past month or so, she had not come to visit and I could tell it was bothering him very much. When Brother Ken Avery asked, "If anyone wanted to stand and share their heart," Brother James stood up, broken and dejected, he began to share that, "His mother had been diagnosed with early onset dementia and Alzheimer's disease." As he explained that, "Only a shell of a person remained," we shared in his pain for his mother. He told us, "That is not my mother anymore; I don't know who that person is!"

We quickly asked Brother James to sit in the prayer chair as the mighty prayer warriors gathered around him to pray for his mother. We prayed with a fervency and desire for his mother as if it was our own. We cried out for the glory of God that night and the Holy Spirit moved throughout the church and you could sense the presence of God. We prayed God would heal our dear brother's mother and bless the hands and minds of the doctors entrusted with treating her. We prayed God would place a peace that surpasses all understanding around Brother James and comfort him. We prayed that a great and mighty testimony would come from this situation that would give all the glory and honor to almighty God.

Within a few days, James' mother had an unfortunate accident and fell and cut her head open pretty badly. Her family made an appointment to see a new doctor to see if something could be done to help her. When they arrived at the doctor's office, they discovered the doctor they were supposed to see was retiring. He had already packed up his office and was about to leave. The nurse apologized and told the family, "She had no clue how James's mother had received an appointment because they had stopped booking appointments several months ago." Little did they know, but God had scheduled this divine appointment! The doctor was a Christian man, so he decided there must be some reason this appointment was booked for him, so he decided to see one last patient before retirement. After reviewing the patient file, he felt she might not have early onset dementia or Alzheimer's disease after all. He had discovered that her medication had been changed around the same time the health issues began. The doctor quickly changed her medication back to what it was previously.

Within a matter of days, her condition improved, and she began to return to her normal self. When we returned to church the following Friday night and heard that the Lord had heard the cries of His mighty prayer warriors, the church erupted in applause and jubilation for another answered prayer for our dear brother in Christ. Brother James shouted out in tears, "God gave me my mother back, praise the Lord!" Our Mighty God had done it again!

OUR PROVIDER

Brother Ken Avery means the world to all of us. We often pray for him, his wife, and all his children and family. There isn't much we would not do for him.

When he first began in the prison ministry, he was preaching at the West Tennessee State Penitentiary. His services grew to over fifty men for several years. Over time, all the faithful men who attended his service were released from custody and returned to their communities. For the next year, Brother Avery preached each week to one inmate named Billy. He began to get discouraged because he was only able to preach to one man. God quickly reminded him of the parable of the lost sheep and said to him one night on the road home, "What if it was me you were preaching to? Would you still go to the prison to preach?" That moment broke Brother Avery, and he remained faithful until one day his own son was convicted of a crime and sentenced to prison. When this occurred, Brother Avery was banned from preaching at the West Tennessee State Penitentiary, where his son was now housed.

Broken, dejected, and displaced, he was questioning God's purpose in all of this until he was invited to attend a revival meeting at the Northwest Correctional Complex in Tiptonville, Tennessee, by Brother Larry Seals from Gulf Coast Ministries. We had an amazing service that night and several men surrendered their lives to the Lord. As he was leaving, our Chaplain, Kurt Gross, was coming in to check on the services. Chaplain Gross asked the unfamiliar face, "What his name was," and he told him, "Brother Ken Avery, it's a pleasure to meet you." Chaplain Gross then shocked everyone by saying, "I know who you are, we have been praying for you to come and minister at our prison for years." A few days later, a service unexpectedly became available, and he contacted Brother Avery. Chaplain Gross told him, "He needed an answer quickly or someone else might take the service." Brother Avery prayed about the opportunity and God told him, "...for a great door (and effective door) and effectual is opened unto me, and there are many adversaries" (1 Corinthians 16:9). Little did he know at the time, but the "adversaries" would come from the church on the outside instead of inside the prison. Brother Avery accepted the Friday night service at the Northwest Correctional Complex.

For more than a year, Brother Avery drove over an hour and a half one way just to share the gospel with us. Over time, this trip became a real burden on him and he desired to move closer to his calling. By this time, the prayer chair had been conceptualized for several months and we asked Brother Avery to sit in the chair as the mighty prayer warriors gathered around to pray for him. As we prayed, the Holy Spirit of God moved throughout the church and you could sense the presence of God. We prayed God would open a door for Brother Avery to move closer to the prison. We prayed God would provide a home for him so he could focus on spreading the gospel. We prayed God would provide for all of his needs according to his riches and glory in Christ Jesus. We excitedly awaited an answer to our prayers.

Within a few weeks, Brother Avery stood up to report that, "A man from his church had approached him about a house very close to the prison and he wanted to sell it to Brother Avery." The house needed some work which Brother

Avery could do once he moved in. The problem was, Brother Avery was leaving his only source of income when he moved and he would not be able to get any type of loan, make a down payment, or ensure him he would be able to pay for it. The man said he didn't care, "God had told him to provide the home to him," so he negotiated a gentleman's agreement for the payments and Brother Avery had a home.

Not only did God provide a home for Brother Avery and his family, but enough financial support began to pour in from supporters of the prison ministry to make the monthly payments. And just because He can, God moved on the heart of the man who owned the home and he canceled the last several thousand dollars of debt and now Brother Avery owns the home. What a mighty God we serve who will provide for all of our needs as long as we are willing to humble ourselves to ask for it in prayer!

A HEALER OF THE HEART

Our prison ministry has faithful supporters all across the country. One of these faithful supporters is a dear sister in Christ named Ms. Lorraine. She has faithfully supported Brother Ken Avery for many years. One Friday night, we arrived at the service only to find a somber feeling in the air. I could tell something wasn't right. We started the service as usual and after a few worship songs, Brother Avery grabbed a chair and said, "We needed to pray right now for our sister in Christ, Ms. Lorraine." He didn't go into much detail, but he told us, "She was in the midst of a slough of despondency and very depressed." We gathered around the prayer chair and began to pray, and the Holy Spirit of God descended upon our church. You could sense the very presence of God as we prayed for Ms. Lorraine. We prayed for a hedge of protection and a spirit of peace over her. We prayed God would lift this veil of depression off of her and show her what His will was in this situation. We prayed God would cause a great and might testimony to come from Ms. Lorraine, giving all the glory and honor to God. We anxiously awaited an answer to our prayers.

Within a few weeks, we received an answer to our prayer. Brother Ken Avery said, "He had talked to Ms. Lorraine, and she was doing much better and the veil of depression had been lifted from her." The amazing part was during this deep state of depression while Ms. Lorraine was praying; God had given her words to a song called *"Just Remember the Anchor©."* She had sent the song to one of our talented musicians, Mark Allen, and asked for him to compose some music for the song.

During some of the darkest times of your life, this song will help lift you up and get you through the storm. I have personally witnessed as this song has helped heal the brokenness for believers who are struggling. Here are the words to this beautiful song:

"JUST REMEMBER THE ANCHOR"©
Written By: Ms. Lorraine King
Music Composed By: Mark Allen

Verse 1:
When your ship is tossed upon the sea... it seems there is no answer...
The waves of life are high and your sense of direction is gone...
When you feel like giving up, and you're weary from the struggle...
Oh, child, just remember, it's the anchor that holds...

Chorus:
Jesus is the answer... He's the anchor of hope...
Jesus is the anchor, and He won't let you go...
Others may fail you when life is dark and cold...
Oh, but you can just remember... that Jesus is the anchor that holds...

Verse 2:
When the storms of life are raging, and you can't find your way...
Your hopes for tomorrow have been drowned, and you feel all alone...
I know that it's easy to think that this is more than you can handle...
But, child, just remember, it's the anchor that holds...

What a mighty God we serve! Not only did He bring Ms. Lorraine out of her deep state of depression, but in the midst of the storm, He used her to write a perfect song to help others battling depression and struggling to find hope and purpose in the midst of their pain. God heard the cry of His mighty prayer warriors, and this song is the testimony. The power of God is in this song and if you ever have the opportunity to hear it performed by Mark Allen, it will transform your life! What a mighty God we serve!

CONCLUSION

There is nothing more spiritually rewarding than being asked to pray for our fellow Brothers and Sisters in Christ and then witnessing God's answers to our prayers. I hope reading about some of the miraculous answers to prayer we have personally witnessed will convince you of the importance and power of prayer. Join with us as we transform the world through the power of prayer!

Chapter 7 You Can Start A Prayer Chair Too!

By now, I am hoping you have been convinced of the importance and power of an effective prayer life. Our Lord Jesus instructed us in Mark 11:17, "...my house shall be called of (for) all nations the house of prayer." The real question should be, is this statement true of your church? Prayer should be a priority for every church! Our churches are a living organism that must be nourished in order to survive. If there isn't an active, vibrant prayer ministry that undergirds the activities of the church, it will suffer and eventually die out.

If this type of prayer ministry isn't already active and thriving in your church—perhaps God is using your time reading this book as inspiration to consider starting your own prayer chair at your local church. Perhaps God is renewing your passion for prayer as a catalyst to inspire change in the way your local church approaches prayer.

The goal of an effective prayer ministry is not to overwhelm yourself by doing all the praying for your church, but to teach other believers how to pray continually and effectively for their families, their church, their local community, the Nation and the rest of the world.

A successful prayer ministry requires leadership, a vision, and a team of mighty prayer warriors willing to carry the burdens to God in prayer. Every ministry at your local church would benefit and prosper if other believers would become devoted to an effective prayer life.

Your local church can start a prayer chair ministry just as we have. The prayer chair is simply a vessel our church has chosen to use as an altar to place ourselves on, as we call the church, to gather around as we unlock the power of God through prayer. We have chosen a chair instead of kneeling before the traditional church alter simply because many of those we pray for are physically unable to get on their knees to pray. However, they are able to sit in a chair as we pray!

For many in the modern church, starting a prayer chair ministry may trample on a lifetime of religious observances of how you have been told we are supposed to pray. We challenge everyone to keep an open mind and test the prayer chair out, because there is no denying the power and effectiveness of the results!

I would encourage everyone who is considering starting a prayer chair ministry to begin praying and talking about it with other believers. The Holy Spirit is calling all believers into a deeper fellowship with Him. And as much as God wants to help our prayer lives as individuals, He wants our local churches to become fervent houses of prayer for all nations. Join us as we continue to cry out to God through an effective prayer chair ministry.

Chapter 8 Conclusion

Our journey started by learning about a gripping story of a prayer chair that is impacting the world. I sincerely pray this story, along with sharing some of God's answers to our prayers, will inspire you to consider starting a prayer chair ministry at your local church. I hope you have learned some important things about prayer that can hinder or enhance the effectiveness of your prayer lives. But I would also like to think perhaps you have learned something new about yourself, including how important prayer can be in your daily life. My aim is that we would all experience the spiritual reward that comes as we learn how to unlock the power of prayer in our lives.

I would like to conclude by praying this prayer over your lives:

Dear Heavenly Father, I want to thank you for this opportunity to come boldly before your throne of grace and pray for my fellow brothers and sisters in Christ.

I pray Dear Lord You would raise up a generation of believers who are unashamed of the gospel, who are willing to stand and fight for God, for their families, for their marriages, for their children, for their churches, and for their communities.

I pray you would raise up an army of mighty prayer warriors willing to boldly call on your name and fight all their battles on their knees while worshiping with their hearts.

I pray that you would raise up a generation of believers who are willing to call on your name, who boldly proclaim Jesus as their Savior, who love, seek, and trust You, and who are willing to stand boldly on Your Word.

I pray you would raise up a generation of believers who will take the fight to the enemy in prayer and not compromise their Biblical values.

I pray you would unite the church and open the eyes of the lost so they might see Your truth through them. In Jesus' name I pray amen!

Don't miss out!

Visit the website below and you can sign up to receive emails whenever Michael S. Dotson publishes a new book. There's no charge and no obligation.

https://books2read.com/r/B-A-OSYOB-BEQMD

BOOKS 2 READ

Connecting independent readers to independent writers.

About the Author

Michael S. Dotson is co-founder of the Break the Cycle Foundation, a nonprofit dedicated to breaking the cycle of multi-generational incarceration. Despite being incarcerated for more than 25 years, he holds a bachelor's of Business Administration from Adams State University. He has dedicated his life to serving others despite his circumstances. He is a self-published author focused on spreading the gospel and transforming lives and communities through prayer.

Read more at https://www.kingdompublishingbooks.net.

About the Publisher

Michael S. Dotson is co-founder of the Break the Cycle Foundation, a nonprofit dedicated to breaking the cycle of multi-generational incarceration. Despite being incarcerated for more than 25 years, he holds a bachelor's of Business Administration from Adams State University. He has dedicated his life to serving others despite his circumstances. He is a self-published author focused on spreading the gospel and transforming lives and communities through prayer.

Read more at https://www.kingdompublishingbooks.net.